Go Hasegawa
Conversations with European Architects

Álvaro Siza
Valerio Olgiati
Peter Märkli
Anne Lacaton &
Jean-Philippe Vassal
Pascal Flammer
Kersten Geers &
David Van Severen

長谷川豪　カンバセーションズ
ヨーロッパ建築家と考える現在と歴史

LIXIL Publishing

Go Hasegawa
Conversations with European Architects

Third published in Japan on January 20, 2020 by LIXIL Publishing.

LIXIL Publishing
3-6-18 Kyobashi, Chuo-ku, Tokyo 104-0031, Japan
TEL: +81 03 5250 6571   FAX: +81 03 5250 6549   www.livingculture.lixil/en/publish/

Authors: Go Hasegawa, Álvaro Siza, Valerio Olgiati, Peter Märkli,
Anne Lacaton & Jean-Philippe Vassal, Pascal Flammer,
Kersten Geers & David Van Severen
Publisher: Jin Song Montesano
Planning, Editing and Producion: Jiro Iio, Hinako Izuhara (speelplaats co., ltd.)
English Editing: Alan Gleason, Christopher Stephens, Susan Rogers Chikuba, Terrance Lejete
Text Translation: Tohru Horiguchi, Haruki Makio
Design: Yoshiaki Irobe, Ryosuke Kato
(Irobe Design Institute, Nippon Design Center Inc.)
Printing: Kato Bunmeisha Co., Ltd.

ISBN 978-4-86480-016-7 C0052
©2015 by Go Hasegawa
Printed in Japan

All rights reserved. No part of this book may be reproduced or utilized in
any form or by any information storage and retrieval system,
without prior permission in writing from the copyright holders.

長谷川豪　カンバセーションズ
ヨーロッパ建築家と考える現在と歴史

アルヴァロ・シザ

ヴァレリオ・オルジャティ

ペーター・メルクリ

アンヌ・ラカトン & ジャン゠フィリップ・ヴァッサル

パスカル・フラマー

ケルステン・ゲールス & ダヴィッド・ファン・セーヴェレン

LIXIL出版

Preface by Go Hasegawa
はじめに ｜ 長谷川豪 _____006

「終わらない」歴史／「ポスト」というイデオロギー／
ヨーロッパ建築家との対話／文化、心を耕すこと
"Neverending" history / The ideology of "post-" /
Conversations with European architects / Culture, the cultivation of the mind

Conversation with Álvaro Siza
アルヴァロ・シザとの対話 _____017

27th July 2013 @ Álvaro Siza's office, Porto, Portugal
2013年7月27日、ポルトガル、ポルト、アルヴァロ・シザ事務所にて

The last Modernist? / Multiplicity in architecture / Legitimacy of the new /
Nature and architecture
最後のモダニスト？／建築の多重性／新しさの正当性／自然と建築

対話を終えて ｜ After the conversation _____046
建築作品 ｜ Architectural works _____048

Conversation with Valerio Olgiati
ヴァレリオ・オルジャティとの対話 _____059

22nd November 2013 @ Academy of Architecture in Mendrisio, Switzerland
2013年11月22日、スイス、メンドリシオ建築アカデミーにて

I do not believe in anything / Architecture stimulates thought /
Ideas, context, and scale / Teaching and thinking architectonically
私はなにも信じない／建築は思考を刺激する／
アイデア、コンテクスト、スケール／建築的に教え、考える

対話を終えて ｜ After the conversation _____088
建築作品 ｜ Architectural works _____090

Conversation with Peter Märkli
ペーター・メルクリとの対話 _____101

20th December 2013 @ Atelier in Hardstrasse, Zürich, Switzerland
2013年12月20日、スイス、チューリッヒ、ハルト通りのアトリエにて

History in contemporary architecture / Expressions of our time /
"Building culture" and synthesis / Conveying experience
現代建築にとっての歴史／時代の表現／
「建物文化」と総合的な経験／経験を伝えるということ

対話を終えて ｜ After the conversation _____130
建築作品 ｜ Architectural works _____132

Contents

Conversation with Anne Lacaton & Jean-Philippe Vassal
アンヌ・ラカトン & ジャン=フィリップ・ヴァッサルとの対話 _____ 143

10th March 2014 @ Lacaton & Vassal Architects, Paris, France
2014年3月10日、フランス、パリ、ラカトン&ヴァッサル・アーキテクツにて

"Cheaper is more" / Largeness and pragmatism /
People's life, and the lightness of architecture / Superposition of times and contexts
「より安いことは、より豊かなこと(Cheaper is more)」／大きさとプラグマティズム／
人々の生活と建築の軽やかさ／すべての時代とコンテクストを重ね合わせること

対話を終えて ｜ After the conversation _____ 172
建築作品 ｜ Architectural works _____ 174

Conversation with Pascal Flammer
パスカル・フラマーとの対話 _____ 185

30th April 2014 @ House in Balsthal, Switzerland
2014年4月30日、スイス、《バルシュタールの住宅》にて

Three reasons to travel / Control vs. the uncontrolled / Double or parallel existence /
A liberating cannibalism / Historical maturity
旅に出る3つの理由／コントロールすること vs. コントロールしないこと／
二重性、あるいは並行的存在／開かれたカニバリズム／歴史観の成熟

対話を終えて ｜ After the conversation _____ 212
建築作品 ｜ Architectural works _____ 214

Conversation with Kersten Geers & David Van Severen
ケルステン・ゲールス & ダヴィッド・ファン・セーヴェレンとの対話 _____ 227

24th May 2014 @ OFFICE Kersten Geers David Van Severen, Brussels, Belgium
2014年5月24日、ベルギー、ブリュッセル、
オフィス・ケルステン・ゲールス・ダヴィッド・ファン・セーヴェレンにて

OFFICE for engineers / What is classic? / Koolhaas and Belgium /
Measuring system and space for life / OFFICE without OFFICE
エンジニアたちのオフィス／古典の定義とはなにか／コールハースとベルギー／
定量化の方法と生きるための空間／オフィスなしのオフィス

対話を終えて ｜ After the conversation _____ 256
建築作品 ｜ Architectural works _____ 258

略歴、編集・翻訳、図版クレジット ｜ Biographies, Editing / Translation, Figure credits _____ 269

はじめに｜長谷川豪

「終わらない」歴史

　2012年の秋から2年間、僕はスイス南部のイタリア語圏にある建築大学、メンドリシオ建築アカデミーで設計スタジオを持つことになった。

　最初のスタジオで、僕は学生たちと一緒に歴史について考えてみようと思った。まずやったことは学生22人全員と建築史を書き換えてみるというものだ。議論を重ね、最終的に彼らとつくったのは長さ6mの巨大な年表だ。11の建築様式（ギリシア、ローマ、ロマネスク、ゴシック、ルネッサンス、バロック、ネオクラシック、アールヌーボー、モダニズム、ポストモダニズム、コンテンポラリー）ごとに色分けされたカードをつくり、それを並べてつくる年表である。カードに印刷されているのは各様式の建築物、建築家、芸術作品などで、その枚数は最終的に1600枚にのぼった。左端がギリシア様式、右端がコンテンポラリーという年表の大きな構造（時間軸）はあるものの、この大量のカードは部分同士の「参照関係」によって組織されている。あるカードを1枚置くとほかの人によってその周囲に「参照関係」をもつカードが置かれる。さらにその周囲にも……と次々に上書きされていく。例えばローマのパンテオン（紀元前25）は平面計画や天井の意匠など、その後の様式においてもたびたび参照され、この年表上に4回登場する。きわめてシンプルなルールだが、上書きがなかなか終わらない。きっと数人であればより厳密なルールを定めてまとめようとするのだろうが、22人の共同作業なのでそうもいかないのだ。最初は3週間でまとめるつもりが、これでいいかなとみんなが思うかたちに落ち着くまで3カ月間が費やされるビッグ・プロジェクトになった。

　学生たちと議論しながら進めるなかで、いくつかの気づきがあった。例えば過去の歴史を「参照する時代」と「参照しない時代」があり、前者はルネッサンスやポストモダニズムなどで、この年表では参照先のほかの時代の色が混ざってモザイク状に表われ、逆に後者の代表格であるモダニズムは比較的ほぼ単色でまとまっている。また歴史はある一個人の意志でつくられるものではないという基本原則は、年

表を22人で同時につくることによって成り立たせた。そしてなにより身をもって気づかされたことは、この作業は「終わらない」ということだ。カードを1枚動かせば水の波紋のように全体が書き換えられてしまう。いくらでも続けられるのである。「終わらない」というとプロジェクトとして不完全で未熟なもののように判断されがちだが、しかしこのいつまでも書き換えが終わらない開かれた歴史、つまり「連続的で積層的な歴史」ということこそ、最も表現したかったことかもしれない。

「ポスト」というイデオロギー

ヨーロッパの学生と話していると、彼らが「連続的で積層的な歴史感覚」を身体化していることがたまに実感できてそれが新鮮だった。そうした歴史感覚は日本ではあまり出会うことがない。と言うと偉そうだが、じつは僕自身にも身体化されていないのかもしれない。どうしてだろうか？

敗戦後に日本が占領下に置かれたときに、それまでの日本の歴史が否定され歴史観が歪められたということはよく指摘されることで、それは大きな歴史的事実なのだろう。しかし戦後の日本人建築家は自分たちのルーツを強く意識することから始めた。坂倉準三、前川國男、吉阪隆正はル・コルビュジエに学んだモダニズムと日本文化の融合を試みたし、丹下健三や篠原一男の初期の作品では日本の伝統が大きなテーマになった（彼らは1955−56年に『新建築』誌上で「伝統論争」を繰り広げている）。つまり戦争による断絶後も、建築のデザインの根拠として歴史が語られていたのだ。しかし、歴史的文脈を無視して古典様式をコラージュ的にファサードなどに引用するポストモダニズム建築が90年代のバブル崩壊とともに終焉を迎えて以降は、日本の現代建築において歴史が表舞台に出ることはきわめて少なくなった。そして歴史が建築のデザインの根拠にならなくなった。

いま日本の現代建築は国際的に大きな注目を浴びている。世界各地で日本人建築家のプロジェクトが進行し、例えば近年のプリツカー賞の受賞者数を見ても世界から大きな評価を受けていることは誰もが認めるところだろう。そうしたスター建築家だけでなく、若手建築家も含めて、小さな住宅作品、抽象性を突きつめた前衛的な空間表現など、日本の現代建築はたびたび海外の建築メディアで特集が組まれている。いま、これほど注目されている国はほかにないのではないか。

もちろん歴史を語らなくなったから日本の現代建築が国際的な評価を受けるよ

うになったということはないだろうが、しかしつねに「古いもの」よりも「新しいもの」を執拗に追い続けることによってほかに類を見ない洗練を果たし、注目されてきたことは確かだろう。国内外の建築メディアもつねに「新しいもの」が生まれ更新される日本の建築シーンを煽ってきた。

　「新しさ」を希求する人間の欲望はかけがえのないものだ。価値観の固定化、画一化を相対化するためにも「新しさ」は人間社会にとって必要なものである。しかし違和感を感じるのは、「新しさ」の希求が既存の乗り越え＝「ポスト」にすり替わりそれが目的化してしまうときである。特に日本の現代建築はたびたび、あたかも師や世代の乗り越えによって歴史が創出されているかのように語られる。知性は集団ではなくある偉大な個人に帰するものであり、偉大な個人史の総和が歴史をつくるとでもいうような感覚。次はどういう建築がくるのか？　次に注目すべき建築家は誰だ？　などと、いつのまにか日本の現代建築は「ポスト」というイデオロギーに支配され、われわれをきわめて近視眼的な歴史観に陥らせてきたのではないか。

　そうした「ポスト」というイデオロギー、乗り越えの連鎖が、戦後日本の現代建築の急速な発展とアイデンティティの再確立に貢献したことは事実だし、僕自身もそうした日本特有のコンテクストのなかで活動してきたことは自覚しているが、これをいつまで続けるのだろうかという思いはつねに持っていた。話題を横にスライドさせ続ける近視眼的「ポスト史観」からそろそろ抜け出して、垂直方向に積み上げていく歴史観について考えるべきなのではないか。これまでの「新しさ」の希求と並走させて、より大きな時間尺度、つまり「歴史的時間」を建築に導入することで、連続的で積層的な歴史観を構築していけないだろうか。そのような問題意識もあって、僕は冒頭で書いたような歴史を考えるプロジェクトをメンドリシオで行なったわけだ。

ヨーロッパ建築家との対話

　現代建築は先の見えにくい状況が続いている。皆で共有できる明確な課題がない時代であるといわれる。そうした状況下においてヨーロッパの建築家が、なにを根拠に建築をつくろうとしているのか、具体的に話を聞いてみたくなった。いま現代建築をつくることと、歴史に向かうことの関係を、いかに捉えているのか。そこでメンドリシオに通いながら、ヨーロッパの建築家に会いに行って話を聞いた。2013年7月から2014年5月にかけてヨーロッパ各地で6本の対話が収録され、それをま

とめたものがこの本である。

　対話の相手となる建築家6組は僕が選定した。収録順に、アルヴァロ・シザ（ポルトガル、ポルト［事務所拠点］／1933生まれ）、ヴァレリオ・オルジャティ（スイス、フリムス／1958生まれ）、ペーター・メルクリ（スイス、チューリッヒ／1953生まれ）、アンヌ・ラカトン&ジャン゠フィリップ・ヴァッサル（フランス、パリ／1955、1954生まれ）、パスカル・フラマー（スイス、バルシュタール／1973生まれ）、そしてケルステン・ゲールス&ダヴィッド・ファン・セーヴェレン（ベルギー、ブリュッセル／1975、1978生まれ）。偶然にも、収録順に並べると約20年ごとに違う3世代の建築家が並ぶことになったので、その順番のまま掲載することにした。どういう時代に建築を学びどのような社会状況で自身のキャリアをスタートしたかということが、その後の彼らの建築思想に大きな影響を与えていることに気づくのではないかと思う。

　質問内容にはフォーマットを設けなかった。話の流れによって僕が思いつくまま質問した部分もあるので全体の統一感は心許ないが、この本をつくる動機になった歴史観、いま現代建築をつくることと歴史に向かうことの関係については共通質問としてすべての建築家に伺い、6組6様の興味深い回答をもらうことができた。また最近は日本に限らずヨーロッパにおいても、社会状況に反応するわかりやすい建築が支持される風潮があるなかで、建築は社会状況にリアクティヴになるべきではないという態度を彼らは示した。「建築は社会をつくると思うか」という僕の質問にもじつに冷静な回答があった。建築が携えるべき時間スケールを見据えて「歴史としての現在」を捉えようとしている。つまり歴史主義に閉じ篭るでもなく、未来志向に邁進するでもなく、過去と未来を同時に「耕して」いるという豊かな感覚があった。

文化、心を耕すこと

　フィリップ・ブドンは『建築空間——尺度について』（中村貴志訳、SD選書、1978、原著=1971）のなかで、いま建築は危機的状況にあり、2つの極端な傾向が現われていると書いている。一方の傾向は「社会学、経済学、工学さらには政治学へと目を転じることになる。それゆえ同時に、建築を問題にすることをもやめてしまう」。もう一方の傾向は「危機を直視することを拒絶する。そして建築を改めて問い直すことも拒絶する」という。40年以上も前のブドンのこの指摘は、まさにいまの建築

の状況を表わしていると思うのは僕だけだろうか。

　そのなかで、ここで6組の建築家が話している内容は、建築から目を逸らさず、そして果敢に建築を問い直そうとする、希望に溢れたものだったと思う。各対話のあとに後記として短いコメントを寄せたので、それぞれの内容についての僕の感想はそこに譲り、ここではひとつだけ取り上げたい。ペーター・メルクリが対話のなかで「building culture＝建物文化」について話している。建築家が語る「建築」ではなく、あらゆる人々がなんらかのかたちでかかわっている「建物」の文化についてである。いま建築家はどのようにして「建物文化」に貢献することができるかをメルクリは自問しており、それがとても印象深かった。

　さきほど〈過去と未来を同時に「耕して」いるという豊かな感覚があった〉という比喩的な書き方をしたが、「土地を耕すこと」を意味するラテン語「colere」を語源に持つのが「culture＝文化」である。英語で「culture」は元来「心を耕すこと」を意味し

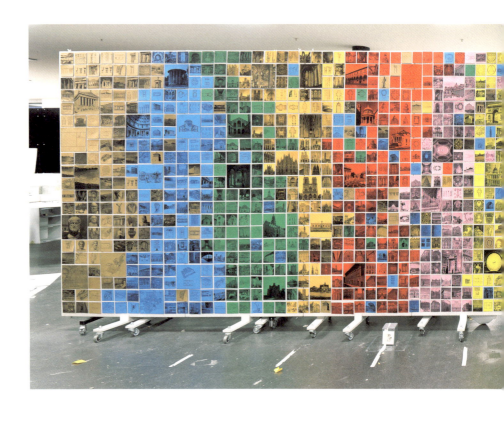

ていたが、その後現在の「文化」や「教養」といった意味になったという。「文化」はまさに自分たちの「心を耕す」ために、つまり精神的、身体的な充実のために、人々のあいだで共有・伝播しそれが内面化していくものである。もちろん「文化」は一個人の発明によってつくられるものではない。

いまあらためて全対話を読み返してみると、メルクリだけでなく6組すべての建築家の言葉には、この「建物文化」が念頭に置かれていたことに気づく。彼らは建築家としての個人的達成を超えて、建物を通して人間がよりよい精神性を獲得することを望み、実践を通してその責務を背負おうとしていた。この「建物文化」が、連続的で積層的な歴史の礎になっているのではないだろうか。

僕たちの時代にいかなる「建物文化」が可能か。僕たち一人ひとりになにができるのか。本書が6つの対話を通して投げかけているのは、この大きな問いである。

Preface | Go Hasegawa

"Neverending" history

For two years, starting in the autumn of 2012, I had design studios at the Academy of Architecture in Mendrisio, an architectural university located in the Italian-speaking region of southern Switzerland.

At my first studio there, I decided to enlist my students in a contemplation of history. My initial project was an attempt at rewriting architectural history with all 22 students. The final outcome of our numerous and lengthy discussions was a huge, six-meter-long timeline. This was composed of an array of cards we had printed up in different colors representing 11 architectural styles (Greek, Roman, Romanesque, Gothic, Renaissance, Baroque, Neoclassical, Art Nouveau, Modernist, Postmodernist, and Contemporary). Printed on the cards were structures, architects, artworks and so on associated with each style; we ended up with 1,600 of them. Bookending this long timeline were Greek style on the left and Contemporary on the right. But most of the cards were generated by "references" to shared elements between styles or eras. As soon as someone posted a card on the timeline, other students would surround it with reference cards, which would in turn be surrounded by others. Thus we were constantly rewriting our history. For example, the floor plan and ceiling design of the Roman Pantheon (built in 25 BCE) were frequently referenced in later styles, so it appeared four times on the timeline. It was a very simple protocol, but the rewriting showed no signs of ending. With fewer participants we might have been able to establish more precise rules for finalizing the timeline, but in a collaborative undertaking by 22 people, that wasn't feasible. What I had originally envisioned as a three-week project ended up requiring three months before everyone could agree that it was more or less complete.

Over the course of the project and the discussions we had about it, several things occurred to me. For one thing, there are "referencing" and "non-referencing" periods or styles. Examples of the first would be the Renaissance and Postmodernism. On the timeline these sections looked like a mosaic of colors from other eras. At the other extreme, the period of Modernism, the ultimate "non-referencing" style, was nearly monochromatic. Also of note: a timeline created by 22 people working at the same time is an effective demonstration of the fundamental adage that history is not created by the will of single individuals. But the lesson that really hit home was that this was a neverending process. If you move one card, it causes a ripple effect—you must rewrite the entire timeline. The modifications can go on forever. We have a tendency to judge "neverending" projects as half-baked or incomplete. Perhaps, though, this was precisely what I wanted to express: a sense of history as continuous, multilayered, open-ended, and constantly revised.

The ideology of "post-"

When talking to my European students, it sometimes struck me that they instinctively accepted this continuous, multilayered notion of history. That was a novel sensation, one I had rarely experienced in Japan. But that may sound arrogant; actually, I had probably not internalized history in this manner myself. Why was that?

It is often said that when Japan came under occupation after its defeat in World War II, there was a rejection of the nation's history up to that point, and its overall sense of history grew distorted. That may indeed be a significant historical fact. Yet postwar Japanese architects based their work on a reexamination of their own roots. Kunio Maekawa, Junzo Sakakura, and Takamasa Yoshizaka attempted to blend Japanese culture with the Modernism they learned from Le Corbusier, while Japanese tradition figured largely in the early works of Kenzo Tange and Kazuo Shinohara (in 1955-56 they engaged in what became known as the "tradition debate" in the pages of the journal *Shinkenchiku* [New Architecture]). Thus even after the interruption of the war, history was still considered a fundamental aspect of architectural design. However, the collapse of Japan's economic bubble in the 1990s brought with it the demise of Postmodern architecture and its collage-like quotation of classical styles in façades and the like without regard for historical context. Since then, contemporary Japanese architecture has only rarely brought history to the forefront. History no longer serves as a foundation for architectural design.

Today, Japan's contemporary architecture occupies the international spotlight. Japanese architects pursue projects all over the world, and a look at the roster of recent Pritzker Prize recipients reveals the global extent of their reputation. This recognition extends not only to a few star architects, but to younger members of the profession as well. Even small residential projects and avant-garde studies in abstract spatial expression are the subject of special features on contemporary Japanese architecture in overseas media. I don't think there's another country whose architecture enjoys such attention these days.

I am not saying that contemporary architecture in Japan acquired an international reputation because it stopped referencing history. But I think it's true that it attracted attention by persistently pursuing and refining, to an unprecedented degree, the "new" in lieu of the "old." For their part, architectural media both at home and abroad have fueled the fire by talking up a Japanese architecture scene that is constantly creating and updating new things.

The human desire for "newness" is something to be treasured. We need the new to ameliorate rigidity and uniformity in our social values. What I find disturbing, however, is when this adoration of the new makes an objective of surpassing what currently exists by replacing it with a "post-" version. Too often it is claimed that contemporary

Japanese architects have created their own history by eclipsing earlier masters or generations. This is of a kind with the perception that knowledge arises not from collective undertakings but from a few great individuals, and that history is the sum of their accomplishments. While obsessing with what new architectural trend will emerge next, and who the next big architect will be, Japanese architecture today has come to be dominated by the ideology of "post-," and that, I believe, has cursed us with an extremely myopic view of history.

The ideology of "post-" and its attendant chain of "eclipsings" undoubtedly contributed to the rapid evolution, and renewed identity, of postwar Japanese architecture. I am also aware that I, too, pursued my career in that particular Japanese context. But I have always wondered how long that tendency would persist. Isn't it time to extricate ourselves from this shortsighted "post-historical" stance, in which issues are perpetually shunted to the side, and reconsider the view of history as a vertical cumulation? By introducing to architecture a larger time scale—historical time—that complements our ongoing quest for the new, surely we can foster a historical perspective that is both continuous and cumulative. These were among the concerns that prompted me to set up the history project at Mendrisio.

Conversations with European architects

The future remains hazy for contemporary architecture. This is said to be an era in which there are no clearcut issues for us to address together. Such are the circumstances that made me want to hear what architects in Europe had to say about the foundations upon which they build their work. How do they view the relationship between history and the creation of architecture today? So I began visiting European architects while working at Mendrisio. Between July 2013 and May 2014 I recorded six conversations at various locales in Europe, and they form the content of this book.

The choices of whom to interview were mine. In chronological order of our meetings, they were Álvaro Siza (b. 1933) in Porto, Portugal; Valerio Olgiati (b. 1958) in Flims, Switzerland; Peter Märkli (b. 1953) in Zurich, Switzerland; Anne Lacaton and Jean-Philippe Vassal (b. 1955 and 1954) in Paris, France; Pascal Flammer (b. 1973) in Balsthal, Switzerland; and Kersten Geers and David Van Severen (b. 1975 and 1978) in Brussels, Belgium. Coincidentally, the order of the conversations happened to group them into three generations of architects roughly 20 years apart in age, so I have reproduced them here in the same sequence. I think it will become evident to readers that the era in which these architects studied and the social conditions under which they launched their careers had a significant impact on their views about architecture.

I had no preconceived format for my questions. Since I often asked questions that occurred to me in the midst of each conversation, there may be a lack of cohesion to the book as a whole. However, I did ask everyone about their thoughts on the role of history in creating contemporary architecture—the question that motivated me to do this book in the first place—and each of them offered distinct and fascinating opinions on the subject. Also, in commenting on the recent trend, seen in Europe as well as Japan, in favor of architecture that responds to social conditions with easily comprehended structures, these architects were of the view that architecture must not be reactive. Their responses to my question, "Can architecture change society?" were also remarkably dispassionate. They see the present as part of history, and keep their eyes on a time-scale that they believe is essential for architecture. In short, they possess a fertile sensibility that clings neither to historicism nor to an exclusively futurist orientation, but seeks to cultivate the fields of both past and future together.

Culture, the cultivation of the mind

In his book *Sur l'espace architectural* (1971), Philippe Boudon wrote that architecture is in a state of crisis, in which context it displays two extreme tendencies. One is an impulse to divert one's eyes toward sociology, economics, engineering, political science—and consequently to cease addressing architectural issues. The other is a refusal to confront crisis head-on or to rethink architecture. I doubt that I'm the only one who feels that Boudon's words, written over forty years ago, perfectly apply to the state of architecture today.

Far from averting their gaze from architecture, the architects appearing in this book steadfastly scrutinize it, and their words are full of hope. After each conversation I have added a short postscript in which I share my thoughts about the content of these chats. Here I would like to mention just one such discussion. Peter Märkli talks about "building culture." By this he means, not the culture of "architecture" as discussed by architects, but of "buildings" themselves—a culture in which people throughout society participate in some way or other. Märkli asks himself what architects today can do to contribute to this building culture, a stance that deeply impressed me.

Earlier I used the metaphorical image of "cultivating the fields of both past and future." The Latin word for "cultivate"—colere—is also the origin of "culture," which in English has come to mean the cultivation of the mind. For culture to nurture our minds, and our souls and bodies, we must transmit, share, and internalize it. It goes without saying that culture is not something invented by a single individual.

As I reread these dialogues, I realized that not only Märkli but all the architects I spoke with shared this concern with "building culture." Having achieved success in their personal careers, they have moved beyond that stage to explore how to provide greater spiritual sustenance for people through their buildings. They view this as a responsibility to be fulfilled through their practice. This "building culture" is what provides, I believe, the foundation for a continuous, multilayered history.

What sort of "building culture" is possible in the age we live in? What can each of us do as individuals? Those are the big questions raised by the six conversations in this book.

Álvaro Siza

27th July 2013
@ Álvaro Siza's office, Porto, Portugal

Álvaro Siza

The last Modernist?

Go Hasegawa   I would like to start by talking a little about Modernism. People say you are the last real Modernist, but of course you are different from Modernists of the past. I mean, your buildings still show us the potential of Modernism. So I would like to start by asking what Modernism means to you.

Álvaro Siza   Modernism is a word used to refer to a period in the evolution of architecture. In that sense, it is finished, because it was followed by Deconstructivism, Postmodernism, and so on. These are classifications. But many values and principles established in the period referred to by historians as "Modernism" can still be used as tools by architects. And the heritage of Modernism has not disappeared. Even in current urban architecture—and I'm not speaking of new production, but the actual structure of cities—you see more Modernism than Deconstructivism, or Postmodernism. So it creates an atmosphere in the places where we live and influences everybody, including young students. I don't think of myself as the last Modernist because my work means more than that heritage, more than following the ways of that period. I see this as continuity in the evolution of architecture.

GH   I see.

ÁS   Another meaning of the word "modern" is "beyond time." In front of my grandmother's house there was a pharmacy (it's still there actually) called Modern Pharmacy. When it was built, it seemed like a modern building for a pharmacy. I don't know how many years have passed, but it's not modern anymore in terms of having a new atmosphere. But on the other hand, I've never seen a Postmodern Pharmacy.

GH   (laughs)

ÁS   Perhaps that's because the values that are related to Modernism are still alive, and many things related to Postmodernism, or the style of architecture known as Postmodern, are not alive—for example, the use of pediments and columns.

GH   That's true. Maybe we could say that Modernism is a sense of pride connected to living in our time. What do you see as the most important Modernist principles?

ÁS   During that period, there was a big change in construction due to new techniques, and tools began to be used to divide space in a structure, which provided us with a great deal of flexibility in organizing a building. On the other hand, many practices from throughout the evolution of architecture were embraced to create new methods and new combinations. This led some aspects of Modernism to be seen as new—things like buildings on pillars, gravitational inversion, horizontal windows, *toit-terrasse*, and free plans—all of the things that Le Corbusier[1] synthesized so well. But these things already existed. Take *toit-terrasse*, for example, all you have to do is think of Henri Sauvage's[2] work in Paris [fig.1]. He frequently proposed several projects that incorporated horizontal elements into the elevations. As for a building on pillars, there's that Rialto market in Venice—it's up on pillars. But it was arranged in a different way because of different needs. Art influences architecture, altering the composition and making it more coherent, but in the end it is continuity, not invention or anything new, just continuity. That is the main characteristic of evolution in architecture.
   Villa Savoye (1929) has an absolutely new image. But if you analyze it, you realize that Le Corbusier assembled things that already existed. I believe this continuity persists, and techniques developed during the Modernist period are still alive. They have just been digested, transformed, and placed in other contexts.

GH   So if we look closely we can detect a sense of historical continuity in Modernism. But haven't there been any breaks in this continuity?

ÁS   In general, no, but Portugal may be different from other countries. In Portugal, there was really no complete Modernism because of the conditions here, the government regime and so on. It was a very closed country, and there were even restrictions about architecture—things like having to conform to an "ideal national style." So we had great Modernist architects, but they didn't produce a lot because the regime wanted national architectural expressions.

Postmodernism was a contradictory movement because it pretended to be connected to history. But at the same time it was like a break from Modernism. It's natural for us to regain aspects of Modernism that we never really had. I remember when some of my colleagues and I were invited to a famous Postmodernism exhibition, we refused to go and issued a statement saying that we didn't understand the term "Postmodernism." We really didn't go. This period called Postmodern in architecture did not last a long time and neither did that exhibition. In my opinion, this is exactly because it attempted to disrupt the evolution of architecture. On the other hand, this is not restricted to architecture—we are all "Postmodern."

Multiplicity in architecture

GH   I visited Santa Maria Church in Marco de Canaveses (1996) [fig.2], and I was surprised by the horizontal window when I sat down. I could see the village through it when I stood up, but I could only see the sky when I sat down [fig.3, 4]. That was very beautiful. Your buildings always present us with new spaces and new sensibilities using preexisting architectural elements.

ÁS   I remember going to Mass with my family as a boy—that was a usual thing—and being impressed but not very happy with how dark the church was because it only had small windows. So I decided I wanted to make a window for that valley, and allow more light inside. At the same time, since you need concentration in a church, you only look out at the landscape when you're standing up not when you're sitting. In my mind, this is to avoid disturbing people's concentration. But you also see high windows. I remember those windows from the same churches when I was a child. I also angled the wall to add depth to the windows like the big stone walls in old churches.

But I added the horizontal window for other reasons. One reason was a discussion I had with a theologian I had the opportunity to speak with about the changes, important changes, in the Catholic liturgy. Part of this is because the Church wants to open itself up to the world, to the people. And probably, because of that, I decided to put in a long window that gives people a view outside, breaking their concentration in the church. And there are other reasons, I am sure. I gave you two, but I know there are others. So we don't design with a single aim—we have our own thoughts, our own memories, things we have seen and spoken about with others, perhaps there are also meetings about our ideas with other people. It is all of this material that results in what we do.

GH   That's an important point. In your architectures, we have a sense of multiplicity. You have never ignored history, nature, art, technology or politics, but at the same time you never seem to depend too much on them. What do you think about this?

ÁS   Yes, yes, that's a good question. I have memories of politics and the relationship between politics and architecture. I remember working in the SAAL (Servicio de Apoio Ambulatorio Local, 1973-77) program in Porto, Bouça, and São Victor. There were many groups of architects who were commissioned to work in different areas. And there were discussions between these groups about what to do during the euphoric period after the revolution (Revolução dos Cravos, 1974). Many people in these groups didn't want to start building because they thought that it was the people who should come up with new concepts for the towns, the new areas. So they didn't build. I even heard one say, "We architects are the hands of the people."

My position was different. I thought that in the end there is no revolutionary architecture. That what we should do the best we could for these people who were living in miserable houses—the small, 4.5-by-4.5-meter, one-family houses in the *ilhas* (Porto's slums)—with all of the possibilities, difficulties, economics, and aesthetics we had. I still want to emphasize the fact that we should provide better conditions for people, and that was not much different from what we were doing then, except for the budgets and political events. For only three years, it was different from regular architecture. For instance, we discussed the projects with people, and began talking not about small details connected to their future homes, but about the towns because they discovered that they needed groups of houses and public buildings. So it was an urban and political discussion that couldn't be designed or placed in a different context.

GH   It's very interesting you didn't choose either politics or the general public, and created a sort of politics with people. Especially Social Housing in Bouça (1977) [fig.5, 6] had always been treated as a solution to problems, but that building was something different, beyond solutions. It looks like a low cost project but their life doesn't look poor, and they seem to enjoy living there even now.

Legitimacy of the new

GH   My next question is about the "new." We always try to produce new things. Why?

ÁS   The "new" is something that we need. We need to change. Many times there is a wish for something new, but even more often there is a demand for it. Because something "new" can be more attractive, and more commercial—and it is also different. There is a great demand for this, just as there are other demands that affect architecture deeply. I told you about the Modernism period in Portugal. There was a demand for nationalist architecture, and many great architects could not develop their own architecture because they were forced to change. So for me what is new, the legitimacy of what is new, is mainly based on the fact that something is needed. There is a reason, not in my own mind, but a real reason to make something in a different way. And that is perhaps what gives what we do its integrity. Integrity is the reason for making a building—that's what makes it look new. Another reason for new things is related to what is local.

GH   Local?

ÁS   Now we are often influenced by globalization, but this is really something very old. Because Portuguese architects were very influenced by what they found in India or in Japan in the 16th century. A new style emerged at that time that made use of a Gothic style of building, but because of this influence it also used a special type of expression called Manuelino[3]. This was new, even though its roots were Gothic. It was new but it wasn't—a new expression that was very influenced by old things. There is at least one town where everything was built in a Manuelino style, and at that time this style was also apparent in towns like Trás-os-Montes and Miranda do Douro. The influence of Japanese paintings, or etchings, and architecture changed everything in Europe, and the basis for modernism is derived from that influence.

GH   I see.

ÁS   For example, when Le Corbusier designed Notre Dame du Haut in Ronchamp (1955) in the mid-1950s, it was like an explosion. For orthodox fans of Le Corbusier, it created a sense of panic because the work didn't contain anything that he had said in his manifestos or books. And then in his last works, like those fantastic buildings in India, he not only dealt with India in a special way, he also made use of local handicrafts. That work, with its very primitive forms, could only have been done by those workers, and he incorporated that into Modernism to make his design. Some people say that it was inhuman and a disaster, and that those big spaces between the buildings were also horrible and inhuman because their scale didn't fit. But some years ago, I had a chance to visit Delhi and when I was in that area near the big fort, the white one I think, I went to Chandigarh. He used this concept for spaces with big distances between the buildings that conform it in Chandigarh. I have no doubt that he maintained this urban concept especially for India. Also, step by step, the town gained more attention. When he arrived in the institutional area, he used that concept of big space. There is a relationship, very direct and very evident, between many towers in North Africa and those ventilation towers in Ronchamp, so I think there is a continuity when there is constant change created by influences that aren't only personal but also cultural.

GH   How about Mies van der Rohe[4]? He tried to disconnect his buildings from the past architectural style.

ÁS   Mies van der Rohe made wonderful big houses in Germany, but he had to leave Germany for political reasons. He went to the United States. Maybe this is a subjective interpretation, but I think he wanted to forget his past because he had to escape to another country; in a way he wanted to cut himself off from that painful past. On the other hand, he discovered an explosion of technology and the power of the U.S. In my interpretation, that is why he chose a method that was absolutely new or at least different in respect to his materials and techniques. He had an opportunity to optimize all of these things, and that's what he did for the rest of his life.

GH   Regarding the local, you are doing projects in China, the Office Building for the Shihlien Chemical Industrial Jiangsu Co. (2014), and in Korea, the Mimesis Museum (2006) [fig.7], as well as in Japan. How do you feel about working in Asia?

ÁS   At this point in time, there is a belief that the future lies in Asia. In Korea, I have had a powerful, amazing experience. It's different from what I feel in Portugal. Because in Korea I felt happiness in the street, and also optimism and competence. I very much liked being there at different times. Japan is a bit different because it is more solidly modern than Korea. Korea had the war (the Korean War, 1950-53), so Japan is more modern, though not in terms of architecture. But the Modernist influence is very strong, so it is different.

And Japan has two worlds. Because you mostly have Western architectural expressions, but you can turn down a narrow street and find these wonderful wooden houses, which means that it is a very ancient and rich civilization that does not change because a new influence suddenly arrives. It is very curious because you don't see a complete fusion, you see two worlds.

In France or in Italy, mainly in southern Italy, they are having a difficult time. And there is not much conviction about what the future will bring. You feel as if people don't see any way out, and that is very impressive.

Nature and architecture

GH   I want to talk next about nature. Two days ago I finally visited and actually swam in your Swimming Pool in Leça (1966) [fig.8]. In the pool, I really felt your special sensitivity toward nature. But I also sensed it in your other buildings like the Faculty of Architecture, University of Porto (1995) [fig.9], Santa Maria Church, and Serralves Museum of Contemporary Art Porto (1997) [fig.10]—your buildings always seem to make a place more beautiful than it was before. How do you create such a nice relationship between nature and your buildings?

ÁS   The first public building I made was the Boa Nova Tea House (1963) [fig.11] when I was 25. I had an opportunity to do it in a wonderful place. The building is on a platform with rocks, which created the contours of the landscape. In a way I created the building almost in parallel to that. I used to sit there when I was making the design and draw all the rocks because I could not capture that with just a plan. In the end, when I finished, I thought the building was too imitative of the natural contours.

Then, I had the opportunity to do the swimming pool, so I tried to start with the idea that architecture is geometry, and nature is organic. I separated the geometric elements in architecture very precisely and concentrated on how they related to nature. I was there for a long time, almost every day, and then I would make my drawings in the studio. One day, I was making marks and thinking that this wall should not be here because it was all alone. Because there was a rock there, I decided to take it to meet the rock. It was rectangular and free-standing, and then I saw the rocks and I thought, "Why don't I use these rocks as the boundary for the swimming pool and only make walls where they are absolutely needed—where the rocks don't solve the problem." Children swim there along the curved wall of rocks [fig.11].

That was what I learned from these two works. I think that I tried to correct this kind of relationship with nature. Rather than trying to make architecture with a natural expression, I tried to find the precise points of contact, then create a whole between nature and the building. Part of my intention was to make it more beautiful! That is the task of an architect, to make things more beautiful. There is a fantastic space made by Bernini in the Vatican. In a text, he wrote about the church and this narrow space, the Scala Regia (1663-66) [fig.12], which allowed access to the palace. He made this wonderful space. He wrote, or apparently said, "The main role of the architect is to make everything beautiful." I was thinking of this example.

GH   I think we Japanese feel a sympathy with your attitude toward nature, which you respect above all, trying to make a place more beautiful before putting up a building. This is my last question. To you, what is "architectural"? You just mentioned the difference between nature and architecture. I always seem to sense your architectural thoughts in your buildings. What is this?

ÁS   Maybe it's all of the things I imagined—nature, place, politics, technique, and so on. It is something that does not reflect any of them directly, but it depends on all of them. Paying attention to what is going on globally, trying to understand everything, and then making something that is an answer to certain needs, but also maintaining a distance from the world and all of those things, so that the work has an autonomy that is more related to the body than to all those things. I'm not trying to defend ergonomics, but it is something that is there. My works are built after considering a lot of things, and being influenced by a lot of things. But I must not look at them and see all of these things because I would be tired immediately. And a building or space is mainly for comfort. It can also be for excitement, but it is not related directly to all those things. It must, however, be completely dependent on those things.

GH Does this answer relate to the fact that as you draw, you think about space through your hand?

ÁS I can control the base of my architecture—the space—and how it is contained—the exterior expression. In sketches, in two seconds, I can become aware of what I am doing. And that is the practical side that defines everything. Having this complete vision from the start, not in the middle of process, allows me to discover when things do not work because I have an idea about everything. And gradually I can give more consistency to that global idea because I am always introducing new information or new ideas very quickly.

The other reason is a text written by Alvar Aalto[5] about his way of drawing and the connection between the hand and the mind. He says that he sometimes came up against an obstacle when he was involved in a project and couldn't go any further. Then he would forget it and go home or go traveling or whatever, and begin making paintings and sculptures, and drawing things without thinking about the problem at all. Then, while he was doing something completely different like that, he would come up with a solution to the problem.

GH Really! You know, I think I'll try that myself. (laughs) Our chat today has given me much food for thought. Thank you very much.

1 —— Le Corbusier: Swiss architect born in 1887 and deceased in 1965. He was mainly active in France and was a driving force behind Functionalist architecture. Major works include Villa Savoye (1931), Convent of Le Tourette (1959), and preparation of the master plan for Chandigarh. Famous for authoring *Towards New Architecture* (1923) among other books.
2 —— Henri Sauvage: French architect born in 1873 and deceased in 1932. Representative works include 26 rue Vavin (1912) and Amiraux Building and Swimming Pool (1924). Both projects have a stepped external appearance.
3 —— Manuelino Style: A late Gothic style developed in 16th century Portugal, during the reign of King Manuel I. The influences of the Age of Great Voyages can be observed in forms derived from fishing nets and seaweeds, as well as exotic American- and Asian-inspired details.
4 —— Mies van der Rohe: German architect born in 1886 and deceased in 1969. After having served as the last director of Bauhaus, he sought refuge in the USA. His oeuvre consisting of rigorous composition using steel and glass is considered emblematic of the International style. Representative works include Barcelona Pavilion (1929) and Seagram Building (1958).
5 —— Alvar Aalto: Finnish architect born in 1898 and deceased in 1976. Best known for his masterful use of light and Scandinavian timber material. Major works include Paimio Sanatorium (1993) and Villa Mairea (1939).

Álvaro Siza

アルヴァロ・シザ

2013年7月27日
ポルトガル、ポルト、アルヴァロ・シザ事務所にて

最後のモダニスト？

長谷川豪（以下、GH） まずはモダニズムについてのお話から伺いたいと思います。巷ではあなたのことを、最後の真のモダニストと呼んでいますが、もちろんあなたは過去のモダニストとは違いますね。あなたの建築物はいまでも、モダニズムの可能性を更新しているように思えます。そこでまずは、あなたにとってモダニズムとはなんなのかをお訊かせくださいませんか？

アルヴァロ・シザ（以下、ÁS） モダニズムとは、建築の進化における特定の時期を指して使われる言葉です。ある意味でモダニズムは過去のものです。というのも、その後にポストモダニズム、ディコンストラクティヴィズムなどの時代が続くからです。これらは分類なのです。しかし、歴史家が「モダニズム」と呼ぶ時代に確立された多くの価値や原理はいまも、建築家のツールとして利用できます。それに、モダニズムの遺産が消えてしまったわけではありません。現在の都市建築──これは新たに生まれているものというよりも、現在の街の構造という意味合いですが──のなかにも、ポストモダニズムやディコンストラクティヴィズムよりもずっと多くのモダニズムを見ることができます。その意味で、モダニズムは私たちが暮らす場所の雰囲気をつくり、若い学生を含めたすべての人に影響を与えているのです。自分のことを、最後のモダニストと考えたことはありません。私の作品には遺産以上の意味があり、モダニズムという時代の手法に倣う以上の意味がありますから。私はこれを、建築の進化における連続性と捉えています。

GH　なるほど。

ÁS　「モダン」という言葉のもうひとつの意味に、「時を超える」というものがあります。祖母の家の前に「モダン・ファーマシー」という名前の薬局がありました（いまもあります）。それが建てられた当時は、薬局にしてはモダンな建物のように思えました。それから何年経ったのかわかりませんが、いまはもう、その薬局に、新しい雰囲気という意味でのモダンさはありません。だからといって「ポストモダン・ファーマシー」という名の薬局を見たことはありませんが。

GH　（笑い）

ÁS　その理由はおそらく、モダニズムに関連する価値がいまも生きているからです。一方で、ポストモダニズムや、ポストモダンとして知られる建築スタイルに関連する多くの事柄は生きていないでしょう。例えば、ペディメントや円柱の使用などです。

GH　確かにそうですね。モダニズムとは、自分たちの時代の生活を誇らしく思うことだと考えてもよいのかもしれません。それではモダニストの原理として最も重要なものはなんだと思いますか。

ÁS　あの時代、新しい技術によって建築構法に大きな変化があり、建物の空間を分割するためのツールが用いられはじめました。これによって建物を構築する際の順応性が大きく広がりました。その一方で、建築の進化を通じて生まれた多くの慣行は、新たな方法と組み合わせをつくりだすために活用されたのです。これがモダニズムの一部の側面、例えばピロティのような反重力的な表現、水平窓、屋上庭園、自由な平面などを新しいものとして見ることにつながるのです。これらはすべて、ル・コルビュジエ[1]が非常にうまく統合しましたが、すでに存在していたものです。屋上庭園を例に挙げると、パリにあるアンリ・ソヴァージュ[2]の作品を思い浮かべてもらえればいいでしょう[fig.1]。ソヴァージュは立面に水平的要素をとりこんだプロジェクトをたびたび提案していました。ピロティについては、ヴェネツィアのリアルト・マーケットのものがあります。柱の配置が異なりますが、それは用途が異なるからです。芸術は建築に影響を与え、その構成をよりまとまったものへと変化させますが、結局それは連続性なのです。発明でも新しいものでもなく、ただの連続性。それが建築における進化の主な特徴なのです。

fig.1　アンリ・ソヴァージュ『Henri Sauvage, Les immeubles à gradins』
François Loyer, *Henri Sauvage, Les immeubles à gradins,* Mardaga, 1987

　《サヴォア邸》（1929）にはまったく新しいイメージがあります。しかしそれを分析してみると、ル・コルビュジエがすでに存在したものを組み合わせていることに気づきます。私はこの連続性は続いていくものであり、モダニストが活躍した時代に発達した技術はいまも生きていると信じています。単に消化され、かたちを変え、別のコンテクストに置かれているというだけなのです。

GH　よく見るとモダニズムにも歴史的な連続性を感じとれるということですね。とはいえ、その連続性がこれまでに途切れたことはないのでしょうか。

ÁS　一般的にはありませんが、ポルトガルはほかの国とは異なるかもしれません。ポルトガルにおいて、真の意味で完全なモダニズムというものはありません。この国の状況や政治体制などがその理由です。ポルトガルはかつて非常に閉鎖的な国であり、建築についてすら「理想の国家像」に従わなければならない、といった制限が設けられていました。ですから、モダニズムの偉大な建築家たちがいたにもかかわらず、政権が国家の建築表現を求めたために、モダニズム建築が多く生まれることはありませんでした。
　ポストモダニズムは、あたかも歴史とつながっているかのように欺くという意味で、矛盾した動向と言えるものでした。しかし同時に、それはモダニズムからの脱出のようなものでした。モダニズムにおいて私たちが経験しなかった側面を取り戻そうとすることは自然なことです。以前、同僚とともに、ある有名なポストモダニ

ズムの展覧会への参加を招待されたことがあります。しかし、私たちはその展覧会に参加することを拒否し、われわれは「ポストモダニズム」という言葉がなにを意味しているのか理解していないという声明を出したことを覚えています。実際に展覧会へは行きませんでした。建築においてポストモダニズムと呼ばれた時代は長続きしなかったのですが、この展覧会の話題性も長くはもちませんでした。私に言わせれば、これはまさに建築の進化を妨げようとするものであったからです。けれどもその一方で、これは建築に限ったことではありませんが、私たちは皆、ポストモダン、つまりモダニズムの後の時代を生きているのです。

建築の多重性

GH あなたの設計した教会《マルコ・デ・カナヴェーゼスのサンタ・マリア教会》（1996）[fig.2]を訪れた際、椅子に腰を下ろしたときに目に入る水平窓に感銘を受けました。立っているときには窓から村が見えたのに、座ると空しか見えなくなりました[fig.3, 4]。あれは非常に美しかった。あなたのつくる建物はいつも、既存の建築要素を用いて新しい空間や新しい感性を表現していますね。

ÁS 子どもの頃、家族でミサへ行ったのを覚えています。よく出かけました。そのときに、小さな窓しかないために教会のなかがとても暗く、そのせいであまり楽しい気分になれなかったことが強く印象に残っています。それで、あの渓谷を一望でき、室内にもっと光を採り入れるための窓をつくろうと決めたのです。それと同時に、教会内では意識を集中させることが必要となるため、景色が見えるのは立っているときだけで、座ると見えないようにしました。人々の意識の集中を妨げないようにするための、私なりの考えです。ただし、高窓もありますよね。高窓は子どもの頃に通った教会のものを思い出しました。さらに、古い教会にある大きな石壁のように、壁に角度をつけて窓に奥行きを与えました。

　じつはあの水平窓を付け加えたのには、もうひとつ別の理由があるのです。ある神学者とカトリックの礼拝式における重要な変化について話をしたときのことです。彼は、教会が世界に対して、そして人々に対して開かれたものでありたいと言ったのです。たとえ教会内の人々の集中力を奪うことになったとしても、長い窓を取りつけて外の景色を望めるようにしたのは、おそらくそうした理由からです。これ以外の理由もきっとあります。いま2つの理由を挙げましたが、もっとほかにもあるでしょう。つまり、私たちはひとつの目的のために設計はしません。自分たちの考えや記憶、目にしたこと、誰かと話したこと、私たちの意見についてほかの

fig.2 マルコ・デ・カナヴェーゼスのサンタ・マリア教会（1996）
Santa Maria Church in Marco de Canaveses, 1996

Álvaro Siza

fig.3 マルコ・デ・カナヴェーゼスのサンタ・マリア教会
Santa Maria Church in Marco de Canaveses

人と話し合うこともあるかもしれません。これらすべてが、結果的になにをつくるかの材料になるのです。

GH　そこが重要な点ですね。あなたの建築には多重性を感じます。あなたは歴史や自然、芸術、テクノロジー、あるいは政治を無視することはけっしてないのに、それらに依存しすぎることもないように感じます。どのようにお考えですか？

ÁS　ええ、それはいい質問ですね。政治について、そして政治と建築の関係について思い出したことがあります。ポルト、ボウサ、サン・ヴィクトルで行なわれていたSAAL（Servicio de Apoio Ambulatorio Local、地域支援相談局、1973–77）プログラムに参加していたときのことです。数多くの建築家グループが異なる分野で仕事を依頼されていました。それらのグループ間で、革命（カーネーション革命、1974）後の高揚した期間になにをすべきかについて話し合いました。これらのグループに参加していた多くが、街の新しいコンセプトや新しいエリアについて考えるのは住民だからという理由で、建設を始めることに消極的でした。結局、彼らがなにかを建てることはありませんでした。「われわれ建築家は住民の手である」と言った者すらいました。

　私の見解は彼らとは異なっていました。私は、結局のところ革命的な建築など存在しないと思っていました。みすぼらしい住居で暮らす人たちのためにできることを全力ですべきだと考えていたのです。イーリャス（ilhas、ポルトのスラム街）にあ

fig.4 マルコ・デ・カナヴェーゼスのサンタ・マリア教会
Santa Maria Church in Marco de Canaveses

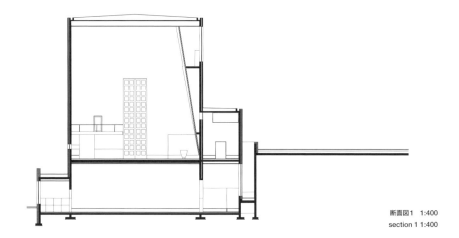

断面図1 1:400
section 1 1:400

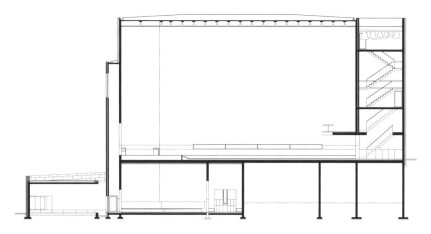

断面図2 1:400
section 2 1:400

Álvaro Siza

fig.5 ボウサの集合住宅（1977）
Social Housing in Bouça, 1977

る、一家族あたり4.5m四方のみすぼらしい住居で暮らす人たちのためにできることを、私たちのもつ可能性、労力、経済力、そして美学をもって全力で取り組むべきだと考えたのです。いまでも、住民によりよい環境を提供すべきだという点は強調したいと思っていますし、それについては当時取り組んでいたこととあまり変わりません。予算と政治的な出来事を除いてはね。3年間だけでしたが、通常の建築とは異なる経験でした。例えば、住民とプロジェクトについて話し合うときには、彼らの未来の家に関係する細かなことではなく街全体のことから始めました。というのも、住民たち自身が住居の集まりや公共の建物が必要だということに気づいたからです。つまり、あれは都市と政治についての話し合いで、そのコンテクストなしには建物を設計することも設置することもできませんでした。

GH　あなたが政治と大衆のどちらかを選ぶことなく、住民とともに一種の政治をつくりだしたというのは非常に興味深いですね。特に、公営住宅は問題の解決策として扱われることが多いのですが、《ボウサの集合住宅》(1977) [fig.5, 6] は明らかに解決策という次元を超えたものになりましたね。低コストプロジェクトですが、住民の生活は貧しく見えるどころか、いまでもそこでの生活を楽しんでいるように感じました。

fig.6 ボウサの集合住宅
Social Housing in Bouça

Álvaro Siza

Álvaro Siza

新しさの正当性

GH　次に「新しさ」についてお訊きしたいです。私たちはつねに新しいものを生み出そうとします。それはどうしてでしょうか。

ÁS　「新しさ」とは、私たちにとって必要なものです。私たちには変化が必要なのです。新しいものをつくりたいと望むことはたびたびありますが、それ以上に、新しいものへの需要があるのです。「新しいなにか」とは、より魅力的で、より商業的なものであり、いままでと違うものでもあります。建築に強い影響を与えるほかの要求と同様、新しさに対しても強い要求があるのです。すでに近代のポルトガルの状況についてはお話ししましたが、当時は国家主義の建築が求められており、多くの偉大な建築家は変化を強要されたことで、独自の建築スタイルを発展させることができませんでした。ですから私にとって新しさや、新しさの正当性とは、主に必要とされているという事実に基づいているのです。それこそが自分の頭で考えたやり方ではなく、物事を違ったやり方でつくる本当の理由なのです。おそらく、私たちがしていることに全体性を与えるものなのかもしれません。全体性とは建物をつくるための理由であり、それによってなにかが新しく見えるものなのです。それともうひとつ、新しさを求める理由として、地域性が関連しています。

GH　地域性ですか？

ÁS　昨今はグローバリゼーションによる影響を受けがちですが、グローバリゼーションとは非常に古いものなのです。ポルトガル人建築家は、16世紀にインドや日本で発見したものに大きく影響を受けていますからね。当時生まれた新しいスタイルにはゴシック様式の建物が使用されていましたが、インドや日本の影響によってマヌエリーノ（Manuelino）[3]と呼ばれる独特の様式も使用されました。ルーツはゴシックですが、それは新しいものでした。新しいものでありながら、新しくないもの——古いものから大きな影響を受けた、新しい表現方法だったのです。すべてがマヌエリーノ様式でつくられた街が、少なくとも1カ所は存在しますし、当時のこの様式はポルトガル北部のトラス・オス・モンテスやミランダ・ド・ドウロなどの街でもよく見られます。また、日本の絵画や版画、建築の影響でヨーロッパのあらゆるものが変化しましたし、モダニズムの基盤はそういった影響から生まれたものなのです。

GH　なるほど。

ÁS　例えば、1950年代半ばにル・コルビュジエが《ロンシャンの礼拝堂》(1955)を設計したときは、まるで突然起きた爆発のようでしたね。それまでずっとル・コルビュジエのファンだった者にとって、あれはパニックのような感覚を生じさせました。あの建物には、彼が公に発言したり出版した事柄がひとつも含まれていなかったからです。そして、彼の晩年の作品、例えばインドの素晴らしい建造物などにおいて、彼はインドを特別に扱っただけでなく、地元の手工芸職人の手を借りています。非常に原始的な形状をしたあれらの作品は、そういった職人たちによってつくられただけでなく、モダニズムを融合させることによって、ル・コルビュジエ独自のデザインになっているのです。あれは人間味のない惨事であり、建物のあいだにある巨大な空間にしても、スケール感が調和していないためにあまりに非人間的だと言う人たちもいます。しかし、数年前デリーを訪れる機会があり、あの巨大な白い要塞の近くの空間に身を置いたときに、私はチャンディーガルに来たのだと感じることができました。彼の使用した、建物同士を大きく隔てる空間の概念は、チャンディーガルにぴったりと調和するものでした。彼がこの都市の、とりわけインドにおける都市のコンセプトを確保しようとしたであろうことは疑う余地もありません。そして徐々に、街は注目を集めるようにもなったのです。彼は組織や企業の集まるエリアでは、巨大な空間というコンセプトを使用しました。北アフリカの多くの塔とロンシャンの換気塔とのあいだには、非常に直接的で明白な関係があるのです。ですから私は、個人的なものだけでなく文化的なものからの影響によって生み出される絶えざる変化があれば、そこには連続性があるのだと思います。

GH　ミース・ファン・デル・ローエ[4]はどうですか。彼はそれまでの建築様式から切り離した建物をつくろうとしましたね。

ÁS　ミース・ファン・デル・ローエはドイツで素晴らしく重要な住宅をつくりましたが、政治的な理由でドイツを離れなければならなくなりました。そこで彼はアメリカへ渡ります。これは私の個人的な解釈ですが、彼が過去を忘れたかったのは、国外へ脱出しなければならなかったからではないでしょうか。つらい過去から自分自身を切り離すための、ひとつの方法だったのかもしれません。その一方で、彼はテクノロジーの急激な発達とアメリカ国家の力の躍進を目にします。私の解釈では、彼がまったく新しいもの、あるいは少なくとも材料や技術という点で異なるものを用いる手法を選んだ理由はそこにあると思います。ミースには、そのような

fig.7 ミメーシス美術館(2006)
Mimesis Museum, 2006

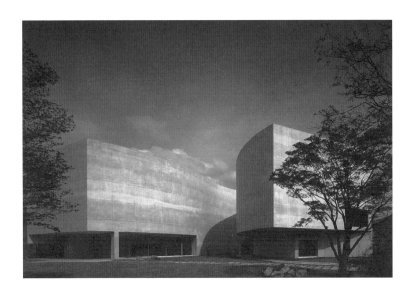

ものすべてを最大限に活かす機会が与えられていて、彼はその後の生涯を通してそれをやり続けたのでしょう。

GH　地域性ということで言うと、あなたは中国《江蘇省の实联化工会社のオフィスビル》(2014)、韓国《ミメーシス美術館》(2006) [fig.7]、そして日本でプロジェクトに取り組んでいますね。アジアで仕事をしてみて、いかがですか。

ÁS　現時点で、未来はアジアにあると信じています。韓国では、パワフルで驚くべき経験をしました。ポルトガルで感じるものとは異なる経験です。韓国の街へ出ると幸せな気持ちになりましたし、自分が楽天的で能力があるようにも感じられたからです。一日のいろいろな時間帯に街へ出かけるのがとても好きでした。日本は少し違って、韓国よりも徹底してモダンですね。韓国には戦争（朝鮮戦争、1950-53）がありましたから、日本のほうが発展しているのですが、日本の建築はとにかく新しいものばかりということではありません。それでもモダニストの影響は非常に強いので、それが違いですね。
　日本には2つの世界があります。大半は西洋的な建築様式なのですが、狭い路地へ入るとそこには素晴らしい木造住宅を見ることができます。それは、新しいものが突然やってきても影響を受けることのない、非常に古くから続いている豊かな文明であることを物語っています。完全には融合しない2つの世界が見られて、非常に興味深いですね。

fig.8 レサのスイミング・プール (1966)
Swimming Pool in Leça, 1966

　フランスやイタリア、主にイタリア南部では苦しい時期を迎えています。そこでは未来がどうなるのかについての確信があまりありません。まるで住民には出口が見えていないようで、それがとても気になっています。

自然と建築

GH　次に、自然についてお話をうかがいたいと思います。2日前にやっと、あなたの設計した《レサのスイミング・プール》(1966) [fig.8]へ行くことができ、実際に泳いできました。プールのなかで、自然に対するあなたの特別な感覚を強く感じました。同じ感覚を、例えば《ポルト大学建築学部棟》(1995) [fig.9]や《マルコ・デ・カナヴェーゼスのサンタ・マリア教会》、そして《セラルヴェス現代美術館》(1997) [fig.10]などの建物からも感じることができました。あなたの設計する建物はどれも、その場所を、建物が建つ前よりも美しくしているように思います。そういった自然と建物の素晴らしい関係を、どうやってつくりだすのですか。

ÁS　公共の建物として最初に設計したのは、私が25歳のときに手掛けた《ボア・ノヴァ・レストラン》(1963) [fig.11]でした。立地に恵まれた環境で仕事をする機会を得たのです。建物は海に突き出した岩の上にあり、周辺の景観は岩によって形づくられています。この海に突き出している岩と並行するかのように建物を配置しました。この設計について考えているとき、私はよく敷地周辺で腰かけて岩を描いてい

fig.9 ポルト大学建築学部棟（1995）
Faculty of Architecture, University of Porto, 1995

ました。平面図だけでは、この設計の全体像をうまく把握できなかったからです。最終的に設計を終えたとき、建物が自然に溶け込みすぎていると思ったほどです。

　その後、スイミング・プールを手掛ける機会を得て、建築は幾何学であり、自然は有機的なものだという考えから設計を始めました。私は建築における幾何学的要素を非常に細かく区別し、それらを自然とどう関係させるかに意識を集中させました。とても長い時間、ほぼ毎日のように敷地へ通い、その後スタジオで図面を描くようにしていました。ある日、印を付けながら、「ここにこんな壁があるべきじゃない、これではこの壁はまったく孤立してしまう」と思ったのです。そこには岩があったので、壁は岩に接してつくることにしました。それから長方形で独立した岩々を見て「ここにある岩をスイミング・プールの仕切りとして使い、どうしても必要な場所、岩では対処できない場所にだけ壁をつくってはどうだろうか」と考えたのです。子どもたちは、湾曲した岩々の壁に沿って泳いでいますよ。

　いまお話したのが、これら2つの作品から私が学んだことです。私はこうした自然との関係を修復しようとしているのだと思います。自然な表現の建築物をつくるというよりもむしろ、自然と建物の厳密な接点を見出し、そのなかで全体をつくり上げるよう努力しました。あるものをより美しくするというのは、私の意図するところでもあります。これはまた建築家の腕の見せ所でもあります。ヴァチカンには、ジャン・ロレンツォ・ベルニーニがつくりだした見事な空間があります。あるテキストのなかで彼は、教会と《スカラ・レジア》（1663-66）[fig.12]と呼ばれる、宮殿へとつながる狭い空間について書いています。彼は素晴らしい空間をつくり上げた

fig.10 セラルヴェス現代美術館（1997）
Serralves Museum of Contemporary Art, 1997

のですが、そのテキストのなかで「建築家の主な役割は、すべてのものを美しくすることだ」と書き、またそのような発言もしていたようです。私も、これを手本にしながら考えるようにしていました。

GH　自然をこのうえなく尊重し、その場所を、建物ができる前よりも美しくしようとするあなたの姿勢に、特に日本人はある種の共感を覚えるのではないかと思います。
　それでは最後の質問です。あなたにとって「建築的であること」とはなんですか？　先ほど自然と建築の違いをお話しされましたね。私はいつも、あなたのつくる建物からあなたの建築的な思考が感じとれるような気がするのですが、ご自身ではその思考とはなんだと考えますか。

ÁS　おそらくそれは、自然や場所、政治、技術など、私が頭に思い描いたものすべてではないでしょうか。そのうちのどれも直接的に反映はされていませんが、それらすべてに依拠しているのです。世界規模でなにが起こっているのかということに目を向け、すべてを理解しようと努力し、さらに特定のニーズに対する答えとなるものを生み出すだけでなく、世界やあらゆる物事からの距離を保つことによって、作品に自律性が生まれます。そこで生まれた自律性とは、頭に思い描いた物事よりも身体に関連するものです。人間工学の肩を持つつもりはありませんが、しかし、無視することはできません。私の作品は多くのことを考慮し、多くのことから影響

fig.11　ボア・ノヴァ・レストラン(1963)
Boa Nova Tea House, 1963

を受けて建てられています。しかし私は自分の作品を見て、そういった数々のことすべてを考えたりはしません。そんなことをすれば、すぐにうんざりしてしまうからです。それに、建物や空間は主にくつろぎのためのものでしょう。刺激のためのものにもなりえますが、私が考慮し影響を受けたすべての事柄と直接的な関係はありません。それでも、そのような事柄に完全に依拠しているに違いないのです。

GH　いまの答えは、あなたがドローイングを描きながら、いわば手で空間について考えるということと関係していますか。

ÁS　自分の建築の基礎である空間と、それを覆う外観の表現については自分で調整できます。スケッチでは2秒もあれば、自分のしていることを意識することができます。そしてそれが実践的側面であり、すべてを規定するものです。こういった完全なヴィジョンをはじめに、プロセスの途中ではなくはじめに持つからこそ、物事がうまく進まない時にも見失うことがないのです。すべてについてのアイデアをすでに持っているからですね。そして私の場合はいつも、とても早く新しい情報やアイデアを取り入れるので、広範囲でのアイデアとの一貫性をだんだんと持たせていくことができるのです。
　それともうひとつ、アルヴァ・アールト[5]が自身のドローイングについて、そして手と心のつながりについて書いたテキストがあります。アールトいわく、プロジェクトのなかで障害が現われ、それ以上先へ進めないことがあるそうです。そん

Álvaro Siza

fig.12　ジャン・ロレンツォ・ベルニーニ《スカラ・レジア》(1663 - 66)
Gian Lorenzo Bernini, Scala Reggia,1663-66

なとき、彼はいったんそのことを忘れて家に帰る、あるいは旅に出るなどしてその障害について一切考えることなく、絵を描いたり彫刻をつくったり、なにかをドローイングしたりするのです。そんなふうに、まったく異なるなにかをしている最中に、問題の解決策が頭に浮かんでくるのだそうですよ。

GH　なるほど、では私も早速試してみたいと思います(笑)。今日はとても深いお話をお伺いすることができました。ありがとうございました。

1 ──ル・コルビュジエ(1887-1965)：スイス出身の建築家。主にフランスで活躍し、機能主義の建築を牽引した。代表作に《サヴォワ邸》(1931)、《ラ・トゥーレット修道院》(1959)のほか、チャンディーガルの都市計画を手掛けた。主な著書に『建築をめざして』(吉阪隆正訳、SD選書、1967、原著=1923)などがある。
2 ──アンリ・ソヴァージュ(1873-1932)：フランス出身の建築家。代表作に《ヴァヴァン街の集合住宅》(1912)、《アミロー街の集合住宅》(1924)がある。いずれも段状の外観となっている。
3 ──マヌエリーノ様式：16世紀ポルトガル、マヌエル1世の時代に発展した後期ゴシック様式。大航海時代の影響から、船の綱や海藻を模した造形や、アメリカ・アジア的な異国風の意匠が用いられる。現存するマヌエリーノ様式の建築物に、ヴァスコ・ダ・ガマの栄誉を讃えたリスボンの《ベレンの塔》(1519)や《ジェロニモ修道院》(1601)がある。
4 ──ミース・ファン・デル・ローエ(1886-1969)：ドイツ出身の建築家で、バウハウスの校長を務めた後、アメリカへ亡命。鉄とガラスを用いた厳格な構成の作品群はインターナショナル・スタイルの象徴のひとつとされている。代表作に《バルセロナ・パヴィリオン》(1929)、《シーグラムビル》(1958)などがある。
5 ──アルヴァ・アールト(1898-1976)：フィンランド出身の建築家。北欧産の木材や光の巧みな使用が特徴的。代表作に《パイミオのサナトリウム》(1933)、《マイレア邸》(1939)などがある。

Álvaro Siza

対話を終えて | After the conversation

2013年の夏、アルヴァロ・シザから対話は始まった。1958年にポルトでキャリアをスタートした、まさに現代建築史を牽引しつづけてきた建築家の重みのある言葉を聞くことができた。

建築の歴史について、シザは「発明でも新しいものでもなく、ただの連続性」だと話した。ル・コルビュジエやミースを「モダニズムの建築言語の発明家」としてではなく、あくまで歴史の連続性に貢献した建築家として語っていたのがとても印象的だった。モダニズムは20世紀前半に世界に広まった一時代のスタイルであるとともに、時代を超越した普遍的な価値観、つまり歴史の連続性を意識しながら現代を表明することでもあるという。後者の意味でモダニズムはいまも続いている。他方で連続性を軽視し、「あたかも歴史とつながっているかのように欺く」ポストモダニズム建築への手厳しさも見せた。

シザの建築は、白い壁、腰壁、光、プロポーション、幾何学と自然の調和といった彼独特のヴォキャブラリーについてよく指摘されるが、それと同時に、完璧さを追求する建築とは異なる、寛容さのようなものがつねにある。彼は対話の最後に、つねに世界に目を向けてそれを理解しようと努めるとともに「世界やあらゆる物事からの距離を保つこと」の重要性を語った。建築にかかわるさまざまな事象に配慮し、しかしそれらに依存しないこと。形式主義的な自律性とは異なる、数々の関係を調停した結果として生まれる自律性と寛容性の共存が、シザの建築を現代的なものにしている。

また日本の現代都市のことを「新しいものが突然やってきても影響を受けることのない、非常に古くから続いている豊かな文明である」と形容したことも新鮮だった。僕たち

I did the first of these conversations with Álvaro Siza, in the summer of 2013. From him I was able to hear the profound words of an architect who has relentlessly scrutinized the history of contemporary architecture since he began his career in Portugal in 1958.

Siza spoke of architectural history as something that is "not invention or anything new, just continuity." I was particularly struck by his description of Le Corbusier and Mies, not as "inventors of the architectural language of Modernism," but as architects who contributed to the continuum of history. In his view, Modernism is not only a style of a certain epoch that spread around the world in the first half of the 20th century, but also acknowledges universal values that transcend time—in other words, historical continuity—even as it expresses its own era. In that sense Modernism continues today. On the other hand, he had harsh words for Postmodernist architecture, critiquing Post-Modernism as "a contradictory movement because it pretended to be connected to history" even as it gave short shrift to continuity.

Siza's architecture is often cited for its unique vocabulary of white walls, low walls, light, proportion, and reconciliation of geometry and nature. At the same time, it always has a quality of broad-mindedness that sets it apart from architecture that strives for perfection. At the end of the conversation he spoke of the importance of "maintaining a distance from the world" even as one strives to understand the world. The idea is to take into consideration all kinds of things associated with architecture, but not to depend on them. What makes Siza's architecture contemporary is not a formalistic

は自分たちの文化や「変わらないもの」を一体どのくらい意識できているだろうか。

さてシザの事務所は、彼の弟子であり親友でもあるというエドゥアルド・ソウト・デ・モウラ（1952生まれの建築家、2011年プリツカー賞受賞）の事務所と同じビルに入っている。シザによって設計されたシンプルな5階建てのビルだ。収録が行なわれたシザの部屋は図面とスケッチで溢れ、窓からは美しいドウロ川とポルトの街並みを見渡すことができた。その日は日曜日。シザ以外のスタッフは誰も来ていなかった。帰り際に、週末もよく事務所に来るのですかと聞くと、シザは頷いた。誰もいない事務所でひとりでゆっくりプロジェクトのことを考えるのがとても幸せな時間なのだと。

autonomy but a coexistence of autonomy and tolerance born of its mediation of many relationships.

Also refreshing was his description of Japan's contemporary cityscape as "a very ancient and rich civilization that does not change because a new influence suddenly arrives." I wonder, to what degree are we conscious of "that which does not change" in our own culture?

Siza's office is in the same building as that of his pupil and close friend Eduardo Souto de Moura (b. 1952), recipient of the 2011 Pritzker Prize. It is a simple five-story building designed by Siza. The room where we recorded our conversation was filled with drawings and sketches, with a view from the window of the lovely Douro River and downtown Porto. It was a Sunday, and no one besides Siza was at the office. As I took my leave I asked him if he often comes to the office on the weekend. He nodded, and said that he treasures the time he spends alone in the office, thinking about projects at his leisure.

Álvaro Siza

マルコ・デ・カナヴェーゼスのサンタ・マリア教会／ポルトガル／1996
Santa Maria Church in Marco de Canaveses/Portugal/1996

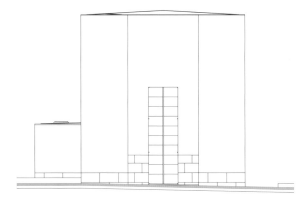

南側立面図　1:500
south elevation 1:500

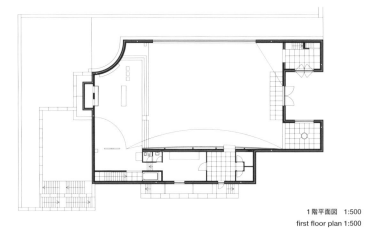

1階平面図　1:500
first floor plan 1:500

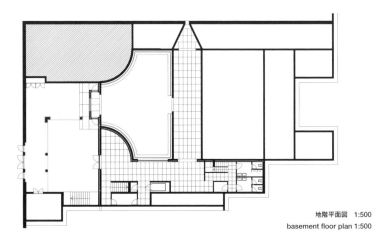

地階平面図　1:500
basement floor plan 1:500

Álvaro Siza

Álvaro Siza

Santa Maria Church in Marco de Canaveses

Álvaro Siza

Álvaro Siza

052

マルコ・デ・カナヴェーゼスのサンタ・マリア教会
Santa Maria Church in Marco de Canaveses

Álvaro Siza

Álvaro Siza

レサのスイミング・プール／ポルトガル／1966
Swimming Pool in Leça/Portugal/1966

Álvaro Siza

Álvaro Siza

レサのスイミング・プール
Swimming Pool in Leça

Álvaro Siza

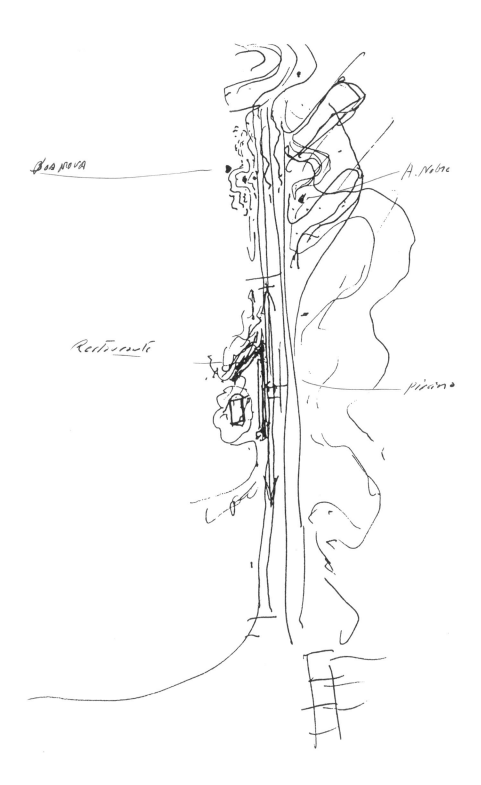

Álvalo Siza

Valerio Olgiati

22nd November 2013
@ Academy of Architecture in Mendrisio, Switzerland

Valerio Olgiati

I do not believe in anything

Go Hasegawa How are European architects dealing with the history of architecture in the current circumstances, when the future of contemporary architecture is so unclear? In this regard, it intrigues me that in several recent interviews you have said, "I do not believe in anything."

Valerio Olgiati Not only do I not believe in anything, my buildings too, are not about belief.

GH It is a strong statement. But more than the statement itself, I'm curious about how you arrived at it.

VO My architecture was born out of the fact that I had to find my own roots. I had a father, a prominent architect[1] with a strong personality that I had to survive when I was young. If I had only worked with my instincts, I would have ended up with a similar architecture, like my father. So I had to find a way to build my own world of values. I had to overcome my past. Instinctively, I like the same things he liked. The difference between him and myself is that he was a man who believed in things while I try not to believe in anything. This is how I started to make architecture. Today I am generally of the view that an intelligent contemporary architect can no longer work with beliefs.

GH But how do you make architecture if you do not believe in anything?

VO   For me personally, when I explain how to make architecture, I always have a picture in my mind. I sit in a boat alone, independent, and I go down a river. The river just goes where it goes and I don't navigate the boat. I just ride in the boat and it sometimes stops here, sometimes there. At every stop there is a reality that I accept for a certain time. This is the moment when I think about a concept for a project in this random and time-limited reality. The concept always has to be basic and it must be possible to formulate it verbally. Sometimes I have a spatial constellation in mind, sometimes it has to primarily express a desire, and sometimes I just want to do something with a certain material, such as red concrete for example. Or for many years I designed skeleton buildings with pillars. They were amazing structures, fundamental, logical, and economical. I could never actually build one. I thought, "I'll just go on and make this type of thing until I can build it. I don't care if it takes 15 years, I'll use this type of building in every competition." I never won, though, so after five years, I decided that was enough and I stopped.

GH   Why did you stop?

VO   I strive for buildings that are as new as possible. The best-case scenario would be if every building I conceive was completely new, a completely new invention. That would be fantastic! I am aware of the fact that I am not really able to conceive something new every time because of various obstacles such as tradition or that my own personality stands in the way of conceiving something new each time. I just try to do what interests me deeply, and interests, of course, can also change.

GH   Do you change in a conscious way?

VO   I usually sense that I have sufficiently dealt with an architectural idea if it becomes too easy for me to conceive of a building. I am always aware of that danger! If I am able to apply an architectural idea as a mechanism because I am sufficiently aware of the logical conclusions of my idea, it loses all appeal for me and I know it is time to stop. I am unable to extend an idea beyond that point because it does not enrich my architectural quest any longer. I don't think that my architecture will ever be in danger of becoming formulaic or repetitive. For me, it is the highest virtue to make new architecture. Newness is very important in order to have a societal impact. And in that sense, newness is a virtue.

GH   Now let me ask you again about your statement, "I do not believe in anything." Modernists at the beginning of the 20th century tried to forget historical styles in order to produce something completely new. What is the difference between you and them?

VO I don't think that the Modernists tried to forget historical styles. Their task was not to create a new style in opposition to history but to create a fundamentally new architecture for a new and better life.

In my architecture I do not claim that it improves anything; it aims to make people's opinions more fluid. I want to make architecture in which people can undertake the fundamental experience of searching for meaning. In that respect, my architecture is fundamentally different from Modernism. Modernism was imbued with idealism for a better world. Today, in a world where values are created by marketing, architects who furnish us with a belief on display are not credible.

GH I see. But do you feel you share anything in common with the Modernists? What about Mies van der Rohe, for example?

VO I think it is really amazing what Mies did. If you look at and study his work, you get a real sense of what the word "master-architect" means. I admire, for example, the Barcelona Pavilion (1929) [fig.1] tremendously, exactly because this building is not clear at all in terms of how the individual building parts perform. I enjoy the Barcelona Pavilion because it is full of contradictions. The contradictions he constructed are intentional. The use of contradictory elements in a building is perhaps an ability I share with Mies.

Architecture stimulates thought

GH All of your buildings look strong, especially from the outside—their façades and their presence. But at the same time they do not say anything. They create a kind of silent pressure and that makes me worry.

VO You know, the problem is that you talk about your individual impression of my buildings and your emotions. So it is already a very personal interpretation, which makes it very difficult for me to answer. Shouldn't we discuss this in a more holistic way? Do you think the buildings are magnetic?

GH Yes, I do. What impression do you expect the façades of these buildings to give? How do you expect them to affect people?

VO For me it is important that my architecture stimulates thought. I don't want to make architecture that one can only encounter emotionally or with feelings. In fact, I believe that an architecture based on such things excludes the viewer.

GH Architecture should stimulate thought?

VO Yes. For example, the Plantahof Auditorium (2010) has an outer shape that does not allow one to understand the entire building organism [fig.2]. From the outside it seems that this building does not need any supports. On the other hand, if we only see the building from the inside, it also seems as if no restraints are necessary. Only when we see the entire building, do we begin to recreate it in our mind and understand why it has supports, why they have the dimensions they do, and why they are positioned as they are. For example, if we enter the auditorium through the rear entrance on the side of the cafeteria, I think we perceive the beams and columns only as decorative elements [fig.3]. This is all the more so because of the specific location of these structural elements in the room, as well as the fact that each of these columns and beams only ever occur there once, and are either very thin or very thick. Usually, one does not see similarities in buildings because it is normal to place the individual parts in a self-explanatory context.

I hope that the individual parts will appear isolated and that in the first moment no accordance will exist between the single components. The insight that the single components and systems concur should grow only with conscious analysis. With only a small degree of accordance, one can prompt people to think about a building. I am convinced that if people are confronted with something that resembles nothing and something that they cannot yet handle, they begin to fathom this and ultimately experience it positively. But my architecture does not have didactic goals. I, however, think that something can only be considered good when it is understood.

GH I see. So, when you use colored concrete, is that intended to stimulate thought?

VO The use of white concrete, for example, expresses to me that a building is an invention, an idea. Maybe here, I can invoke the term "enlightenment." These buildings are inventions, non-contextual buildings that have developed from within themselves. Those constructions in turn that are cast in a red-brown concrete, stand in reference to the fact that the structures grow literally from the ground. I still would not describe my red-brown concrete buildings as necessarily contextual in the familiar sense. However, there are buildings that are not only conceived, so they are not only created in the mind of one person. These works do not appear to be pure inventions that I have made. I believe there is a distinction between these two types—a more earth-related architecture, and an architecture that is related to enlightenment, which is more of an invention, an abstraction, something non-referential. Yes, perhaps I can say that one type has a non-referential character and the other is more referential.

Ideas, context, and scale

GH   I was surprised at the sense of scale of your buildings. The ceiling height, the doorknobs—they look 1.2 times the size of those of regular buildings. I've never seen another contemporary architect like you. For example, Kazunari Sakamoto's[2] buildings are 0.9 times smaller than regular buildings, and the elements, like the height of the roof and the furniture, are always a little bit smaller than average, which creates a unique quality overall.

You might be unconscious of this sense of scale. But it makes your buildings appear majestic—they look like temples. Regardless of the program, your buildings have a temple-like quality about them. And from this, I can sense how you think about architecture.

VO   The sense of scale you are talking about has little to do with the fact that my projects are bigger or smaller than regular buildings. Some of my buildings are exactly as big as the buildings that stand next to them. For instance, we had to rebuild the exact volume of the existing barn for Atelier Bardill (2007) [fig.4] in order to get permission to build it from the community. The existing barn, which had been constructed by farmers a long time ago, was the basis for our project and every single aspect had to be rebuilt. We had to do the same thing with my office in Flims. I think we should talk more talk about how these buildings create their own context while not being what is commonly referred to as "contextual." This is what I think you mean by "sense of scale." I am not interested in a "contextual" approach. There is an architecture that is fundamentally non-contextual which emerges from itself—an architecture that does not develop from the context. I think that an architect, who is developing a project based on an idea, may not respond to context. A temple is never contextual. The stables, for example, that surround my house are not contextual. In this zone, all stables are 12/12 or 12/18 meters. The size and shape are based on the number of cows and amount of hay that is required in order to survive the winter. For farmers, there is no romantic view to context. And yet, these stables create a wonderful context. My buildings create a context. So when I develop my buildings, I want to find criteria that come directly out of an idea while not being abstractions of the surroundings or from anything else.

Take, for example, the Swiss National Park Visitor Center in Zernez (2008) [fig.5, 6]. The idea for this building called for four windows with equal dimensions in each room. If you compare the relationship between the walls and windows, you will find that the walls are about 80 percent of the building. But the building still looks very public. The building does not look like a residence or an administrative office. When I think about an idea, I only differentiate between houses, working places, and public spaces—just between those three types.

Valerio Olgiati

GH   Only three! (laughs)

VO   Yes. (laughs)

GH   It's interesting. For example, the space inside the School in Paspels (1998) [fig.7, 8] is quite high for children. But it creates a majestic atmosphere so that when children enter the building, it gives them a rich experience—like a temple.

VO   Here we could talk for hours to find out what you think a school and what a temple is. For me Paspels is the prototype of a school, rather than a temple. That school was a pure invention. The building is more or less a cube that has, in its midst, a central space. If you enter the building you arrive at this central space and you can look in every direction from the inside out. You could put this building anywhere you want and it would work in essentially the same way. So, the setting of the building is not that important on that primary level of what the building does and what it is.

It is this kind of generality that I find interesting in my architectural practice: the generality and what to do with that generality. Because that kind of generality in architecture demands the invention of building parts that are not based on certain contextual types and motifs as they exist in the vicinity of the building site. And again, these inventions could exist anywhere.

GH   So your aim is making things that are free from function?

VO   Let me explain this a bit more clearly. The function within a room is not the force that causes me to make a space one way or another. I'm not a functionalist. But every space has a function—either programmatic or architectonic. What I mean by "function" is related to the ontological foundation of a room. It is a quest to find out why a room should be one specific way and no other. I am focusing more and more on this question of the nature of rooms.

GH   That's interesting. And it's true there is an architectonic quest in all of your buildings. You focus strongly on that aspect and that gives the spaces a kind of tension. What do you think about my suggestion of the temple-like quality in your buildings?

VO   I do not want to use the word "temple" in comparison to my buildings. What interests me much more is the idea of a temple—its non-referentiality. Let me explain the difference between the non-referential and the abstract with an example from past architecture that is an important part of my own aims as an architect. The temples at Angkor Wat in Cambodia [fig.9] are an abstraction, while the Mayan temples at Tikal in Guatemala [fig.10] are an example of an invented and non-referential architecture. If it is an abstraction, there is a point of departure and a genealogy, while an invention does not have such ancestry. With an invention, I define something that is non-referential in regard to its formal properties as well as to its content. An abstraction is always the discourse of an origin that is subsequently transformed. The temples of Angkor Wat are a depiction of shamanistic beliefs that are the basis of Buddhism. The subject is always those mountains, the peaks of the Mount Meru and the Himalayas, which are the seats of the gods. What we see at Angkor Wat is the abstraction of that image. That is why the temples look like mountains; these buildings are abstracted depictions of nature as the builders saw it. The Mayans, on the other hand, do not depict anything with their temples. It is completely unknown where the shapes originated from. It is not possible to trace their origins to find out why the temples look the way they do. Mayan temples are a pure invention of the Mayan power of imagination. I am fascinated by a society that is able to construct an artifact that is not an abstraction. The Greek temple is an abstraction of a house, dome structures are an abstraction of Heaven, and Asian temples are abstractions of mountains, but the Pre-Columbian temples of the Mayans are an intellectual projection of something people imagined.

The difference between the two is important for me because I would like to work like the Mayans did. I would like to make something that is radically new, something that is invented. I am aiming for an architecture that has no origins and is thus non-referential.

GH   By non-referential architecture, do you mean pure architecture?

VO   Architecture which is able to exist on its own, without external arguments or even references to a belief. Pure architecture as you will.

Teaching and thinking architectonically

GH   You have been a teacher for ten years in Mendrisio. What is your view of education and what is the relationship between your practice and your role as a professor?

VO   Here at the university I am neutral. It is also a place where I can relax.

GH   Relax?

VO   Yes, because when I work in the office, thinking about architecture is always a fight—I have to be strategic. At the university, I am more at home with architecture. It is not very important to fight. I can play more freely here, without strategies or tactics. What is important here is that I can say whatever I want. In the office I can also say what I want, but I cannot do whatever I want. Teaching is like therapy, like a holiday. I like it very much. And I especially like Mendrisio because there are students from all over the world. I like these people with different ideas, different backgrounds. It helps me understand the world better.

GH   Could you tell me your thoughts about the meaning of architectural education today?

VO   I cannot understand the total neglect of the fundamentally architectonic within academia. I am not interested in taking operations and mechanisms from other disciplines such as art, mathematics, sociology, and adapting complex transfigurations of those extra-architectural operations to somehow relate them back to architecture. Frankly, this is illogical. It is not that architecture cannot be innovative and expand its boundaries, but I doubt that such an expansion of architecture will ever come by means of extra-architectural content or operations. I am convinced that the only legitimate growth lies in architecture that grows out of itself. I wonder why so many architects have to step outside of architecture to find something that they consider worthwhile in order to allow them to conceive of architecture.

I am particularly dumbfounded by architecture education and wonder why all of these phenomenological considerations are seen as so important. The entire phenomenological approach to architecture is based outside the discipline itself and this approach is a short-lived trend that will fail to renew or enrich the discipline. I am not denying that architecture has a phenomenological dimension. This dimension has always been a part of architecture, but I do not understand why the entire making of architecture has to be subjected to a phenomenological approach. Is it so difficult to see that an architect who conceives of architecture phenomenologically has already proven himself to be too corrupt to deal with phenomena in a fundamental way, as the phenomenological approach demands? The fact that an architect declares such a credo is evidence that the necessary cultural innocence for such a phenomenological position already has been intellectualized. This phenomenological approach has the same problem as Minimal Art. Minimal Art was also so focused on not trying to depict anything that that became its reference. These are all contorted constructions that are extra-architectural and, I repeat, pointless for architecture. Perhaps I single out the Minimalist and associated phenomenological approaches more than other extra-architectural influences because sometimes I find my architecture labeled as "Minimalism," which is a gross misinterpretation. I think architectonically through and through! To think architectonically is extraordinarily rich. I enjoy it! As a matter of fact, my own ambition is to expand architecture in such a way that there will be absolutely no reference: I dream of pure architecture!

GH   At the design stage of your projects, how do you capture the concept and the moment where they make sense?

VO   The question of sense is totally dependent on the time and the culture you are living in. In Asian countries, the question of sense is probably more important than here in the Western world. I'm not interested in this question because it has to do again with a personal or social interpretation. But I believe that there is a fundamental different way of doing architecture. Perhaps it is this distinction that makes certain buildings understandable and others not. Basically, I think there are two categories of architects: the assembler and the divider. I see myself as a divider. An assembler, or perhaps a composer, is more animalistic and operates with less mental effort. The divider, on the other hand, takes on a more complex task. He works strategically and defines a target. His architecture begins with a certain universal form, which mainly reflects the idea. He then divides this idea until it can exist as a structure. When you start from an idea, everything has to fit—everything from the constructional to the spatial, from the use to the expression. The most challenging task is to design a single object out of this process.

1 —— Rudolf Olgiati: Swiss architect born in 1910 and deceased in 1995. He designed many residences and facilities for the Swiss alpine village of Flims.
2 —— Kazunari Sakamoto: Japanese architect born in 1943. Professor at the Tokyo Institute of Technology from 1991 to 2009. Representative works include House in Sanda (1969), Common City Hoshida (1992), and House SA (1999).

ヴァレリオ・オルジャティ

2013年11月22日
スイス、メンドリシオ建築アカデミーにて

私はなにも信じない

長谷川豪（以下、GH）　先が見えにくい現代建築のいまの状況において、ヨーロッパの建築家たちはどのように建築の歴史と向き合っているのでしょう？　あなたは最近のインタヴューで「私はなにも信じない」と何度か答えておられて、非常に興味深く感じました。

ヴァレリオ・オルジャティ（以下、VO）　私自身がなにも信じないというだけではなく、私の建物も信念とは関係がないのです。

GH　断言されますね。その考え自体も興味深いのですが、まずはどういった経緯でそう考えるようになったのかお訊かせください。

VO　私の建築は、自分のルーツを探さなければならないというところから始まっています。父は有名な建築家[1]だったため、私が若かった頃は父の強い個性にさらされていました。もしも、特になにも考えずに仕事をしていれば、私は父と似たような建築をつくっていたことでしょう。ですから、自分の価値観を模索し、独自の道を歩まなければならなかったのです。直感的な部分では、私は父と趣向が似ています。しかし、父は物事を信じ、私はなにも信じようとしないところに違いがあります。私はそんなふうにして建築をつくりはじめました。現代の聡明な建築家は、信念だけでは仕事ができなくなったというのが、いまの私の基本的な考えです。

GH　なにも信じないで、建築をどのようにつくるのですか。

VO　個人的には、建築をどうつくるかを説明するとき、つねに心のなかに浮かぶイメージがあります。ボートにひとりで乗りこみ、川をあてどもなく下っているイメージです。ボートを漕ぐわけでもなく、川の流れに任せます。私はただ乗っているだけです。所々で止まることもあります。止まったときに、現実を受け入れることとなります。つまり、偶然に左右され、時間制限もある現実世界でのプロジェクトとして、コンセプトを考えるのです。コンセプトは基本的なことであり、言葉で説明できるものでないといけません。空間の集合のイメージを持っている場合もあれば、願望を表現することもあるし、赤褐色のコンクリートのような特定の材料を使いたいという場合もあるでしょう。あるいは、私は支柱のあるスケルトンビルを何年間も設計してきました。そのスケルトンビルは素晴らしい構造で、基本的かつ合理的で、経済的でもありました。とはいえ、それらが実際に建つことはありませんでしたが。「15年かかっても構わないから、実現するまでこのタイプの建物を追求しよう。すべてのコンペでスケルトンビルを使おう」と考えていました。しかし、結局コンペで勝つことはできず、5年後に、もうやめようと決心したのです。

GH　なぜやめたのでしょうか。

VO　私はできるだけ新しい建築に取り組みたいのです。最高なのは、思いついた建物がいままでにないもので、新たな発明であることです。それができたらなんと素晴らしいことでしょう！　しかし実際には、伝統や自分の性格が邪魔をしたりするので、いつも新しいものを思いつけるわけではありません。私は単に、自分が深く興味を持ったことに取り組みたいだけなのです。もちろんその興味が変わることもあります。

GH　それは意識的に変えるのですか？

VO　ある建物を簡単に考案できるのであれば、その建築的アイデアはもう十分に汲みつくされたように感じるのです。そうした危険性にはいつも気をつけています。もし自分の建築的アイデアがどういう結論に至るかを十分論理的に理解していて、それを仕組みとして適用できるというのであれば、そのアイデアは私にとって魅力がまったくなくなってしまっていて、手放す潮時だと感じるのです。建築的な探求を豊かにしてくれるものでなければ、アイデアをそこから発展させることはで

きません。私の建築が、決まりきったものや同じものの繰り返しになってしまうということはないでしょう。私にとって一番の美徳は新しい建築をつくることで、新しさというのは社会的なインパクトを与えるがゆえに非常に重要です。新しさは美徳なのです。

GH　それではあなたの言う「私はなにも信じない」という姿勢についてですが、モダニズムの建築家たちは20世紀の初め、完全に新しいものをつくるために歴史的なスタイルをすべて断ち切ろうとしました。あなたと彼らモダニストたちの違いはなんでしょうか。

VO　私は、モダニストたちが歴史的なスタイルを断ち切ろうとしたとは思いません。モダニストたちの目的は、歴史に反して新しいスタイルをつくることではありませんでした。新しくて、よりよい生活のために、根本的に新しい建築を確立しようとしたのです。私は自分の建築によってなにかが改善するとは考えていません。私の建築は、人々の意見をより流動的にすることを目指しています。人々が意味を探求するための本質的な実験ができる建築をつくりたいのです。ですから、モダニズム建築と私の建築は根本的に違います。モダニズムはよりよい世界のための理想主義に満ちています。モノの価値がマーケティングによって決まる現代社会において、信念を並べたてている建築家は信用できません。

GH　なるほど。しかしあなた自身は、モダニストとのなんらかの共通点があると思っていますか？　例えばミース・ファン・デル・ローエはどうでしょう。

VO　ミースの功績は本当に驚嘆すべきものです。彼の建築を見れば、「マスター・アーキテクト」の真の意味がわかるでしょう。例えば、私は《バルセロナ・パヴィリオン》(1929) [fig.1]に畏敬の念を抱いていますが、その理由は、建物の各要素がどのように機能しているかということが、まったく明らかではないからです。《バルセロナ・パヴィリオン》は矛盾に満ちているからこそ楽しめるのです。その矛盾はミースによって意図的につくられたものです。建物に矛盾した要素を用いるという点は、もしかしたらミースと私の共通した能力なのかもしれません。

建築は思考を刺激する

GH　あなたの建物はいずれも、強さを備えているように見えます。特に外観、つ

fig.1 ミース・ファン・デル・ローエ《バルセロナ・パヴィリオン》(1929/1986再建)
Mies van der Rohe, Barcelona Pavilion, 1929 (1986 reconstruction)

まりファサードや存在感からそのような印象を受けます。しかし同時に、あなたの建物は主張もしません。無言の圧力のようなものを感じさせるのです。

VO　ええと、あなたが述べているのは、私の建物に対する個人的な印象や感情ですね。その時点できわめて個人的な解釈に属する事柄ですから、私にとっては非常に答えにくいものです。もう少し全体論的な話をしませんか？　私の建築に、なにか磁場のようなものを感じるということですか？

GH　まさにそうです。あなたはそうした建物の外観の印象になにを期待していますか？　そして、それが人々にどのような影響を与えることを考えているのでしょうか。

VO　私にとっては、自分の建築が思考を刺激することが重要です。人が感情や感覚だけで対峙できるような建築をつくりたくはありません。むしろ、そういう建築は観る人のことをなにも考えていないと思っています。

GH　思考を刺激する建築ですか。

VO　はい。例えばプランタホフでのプロジェクト《プランタホフ農業学校の講堂》(2010)では、建物の全体像が外見だけではわからないようになっています [fig.2]。外

Valerio Olgiati

fig.2 プランタホフ農業学校の講堂（2010）
Plantahof Auditorium, 2010

Valerio Olgiati

Valerio Olgiati

fig.3 プランタホフ農業学校の講堂
Plantahof Auditorium

からは支柱が必要ないように見えます。一方、建物のなかだけを見ても、なんの制約も必要としていないように見えます。建物全体を把握したときにはじめて、支柱の意味や、それぞれの寸法や配置の意味が理解できるようになるのです。例えば、食堂の側の裏口から講堂に入ると、梁や柱が単に装飾的な要素にしか見えないと思います [fig.3]。構造要素の配置が独特であるため、梁や柱を目にするのは一度だけですし、それらは非常に細いか太いかのどちらかですから、一層そう感じるでしょう。通常は個々の部分が自明のコンテクストに基づいて配置されているので、別々の建物に類似性を感じることはありません。

　私は各部分が独立し、最初はそれぞれの構成要素になんの調和も存在していないかのように見えるよう意図しているのです。各要素と全体のシステムが一致しているということは、意識的に分析してみてはじめてわかることです。ほんのわずかに調和の度合いを示すだけで、人々が建物のことを考えるように促すことができます。これまで見たことがなくて判断できないものに直面すると、人は考えはじめ、最終的には積極的に体験するようになると確信しています。私の建築には教訓的な目標はありませんが、強いて言えば、理解しなければそのよさがわからないようなものと言えるでしょうか。

GH　例えば着色コンクリートの使用も思考を刺激するためということでしょうか。

VO　白色のコンクリートを使うのは、その建物がひとつの発明であり、ひとつの

アイデアであることを表現するためです。そうですね、「啓発」という言葉が適当でしょうか。独自の、コンテクストに依らない建物であり、発明です。一方、赤褐色のコンクリートは、この構造物が文字通り地面から生え出ていることと関連しています。赤褐色のコンクリートからなる私の建物は、従来の意味合いでのコンテクストに基づいたものではありません。しかし、考えだけに基づく、つまりひとりの頭のなかで考え出されただけの建物でもありません。このような建築は、私がつくる純粋な発明とは言えないと思います。建築には2つのタイプ、より地球環境との関係を意識した建築と、より発明的で抽象的な、そして参照項を持たないような、啓発にかかわる建築があると考えています。つまり、参照項によって区別されるのだと思います。

アイデア、コンテクスト、スケール

GH あなたの建物のスケール感には驚かされました。天井高やドアノブなどが通常のものに比べ1.2倍ほど大きいのです。あなたのような建築家は、現代にはあまりいないと思います。例えば坂本一成さん[2]の建築は、言うなれば通常に比べて0.9倍の大きさで、屋根の高さや家具などの要素がややこぢんまりとしており、それが空間の質につながっています。あなたはこのようなスケール感を意識していないかもしれません。しかし、プログラムや用途にかかわらずあなたのスケール感は建物を堂々と見せ、なにか神殿のようにも見えます。このことから、建築に対するあなたの思想が窺える気がします。

VO 私のプロジェクトが通常の建物に比べて大きかったり小さかったりしたとしても、いまあなたがおっしゃったようなスケール感というのはあまり関係がありません。私の建築のなかには、隣に建っている建物とまったく同じ大きさのものもあります。例えば、《リナード・バルディルのアトリエ》(2007) [fig.4]では、地域の理解を得るために、以前あった納屋とまったく同じヴォリュームにする必要がありました。大昔に農夫によって建てられた納屋がプロジェクトの基礎となっていて、それをあらゆる面で再構築する必要がありました。フリムスにある私の事務所にしてもそうです。これらの建物は独自のコンテクストをつくりだしており、一般的に言われるところの「コンテクストに基づいた」ものではないということについて、もう少しお話したほうがいいかもしれませんね。おそらくそのことが、あなたの言う「スケール感」でしょう。私はコンテクストに基づいたアプローチには関心がありません。建築には、本質的にコンテクストとは無関係に独自のものとして現われる

fig.4 リナード・バルディルのアトリエ（2007）
Atelier Bardill, 2007

Valerio Olgiati

fig.5　スイス国立公園ビジターセンター(2008)
Swiss National Park Visitor Center, 2008

ものがあります。つまり、コンテクストから生み出されてはいない建物です。私のように、あるアイデアをもとにプロジェクトを展開していくような建築家は、コンテクストには反応しないかもしれません。神殿はコンテクストに基づくものではありえません。私の家の周辺にある家畜小屋も、コンテクストに基づくものではありません。この家畜小屋はすべて12×12m、もしくは12×18mです。小屋の大きさと形状は、牛の数と、冬を乗り越えるために必要な干し草によって決められています。農夫には、コンテクストに対するロマンチックな考えはありません。それでも、家畜小屋は素晴らしいコンテクストとなります。私の建物も同じです。ですから、私が建物をつくるとき、周囲のコンテクストやなにかほかのものから抽出したものではない、アイデアから直接的に導き出されるような基準を見つけたいのです。

　《スイス国立公園ビジターセンター》(2008) [fig.5, 6]を例にとりましょう。各部屋の4面に、同じ大きさの窓がある建物というアイデアです。壁と窓の関係性を比較すると、壁が建物の80％を占めていることがわかります。しかし、建物は公共建築のように見えるのです。住宅やオフィスのようには見えません。私が構想を練るときに区別するのは、住宅、オフィス、公共空間の3つだけです。

GH　3つだけですか！(笑)

VO　はい(笑)。

fig.6 スイス国立公園ビジターセンター
Swiss National Park Visitor Center

Valerio Olgiati

Valerio Olgiati

fig.7 パスペルスの小学校（1998）
School in Paspels, 1998

GH　とても興味深いですね。例えば《パスペルスの小学校》(1998) [fig.7, 8]内の空間において、天井は子どもにとっては非常に高く設計されています。神殿のような堂々とした雰囲気があり、建物に入ってみると、子どもたちは豊かな経験をしていることがわかります。

VO　あなたにとって学校と神殿がなんであるかという話を訊いていくと何時間も経ちそうですね。私にとって《パスペルスの小学校》は神殿というより、あくまでも学校のプロトタイプです。《パスペルスの小学校》は純粋な発明といえる建物なのです。建物自体はほぼ立方体で、その中心に空間を内包しています。中央の空間に入ると、すべての方向に対して、内から外を見渡すことができるのです。この建物をそのままどこか別の場所に配置したとしても、基本的にその機能は変わりません。建物がどのように機能するか、なんの建物であるかを考えるうえで、建物がどこに配置されるかということはさほど重要ではありません。
　私の建築的な実践において興味深く感じているのは、このような普遍性です。普遍性それ自体についても、また、その普遍性をどのように扱うのかということについても関心があります。普遍性によって、建築家には、現場の周辺に存在する特定のコンテクストやモティーフに基づかない独自の建物要素を発明することが求められるからです。先ほども言ったとおり、こういった発明はどのような場所でもありえるのです。

Valerio Olgiati

fig.8 パスペルスの小学校
School in Paspels

GH　つまりあなたが目指しているのは、機能から自由になったものをつくるということですか？

VO　もう少しわかりやすく説明しましょう。私にとって、部屋の機能というものは、いかなる意味においても、空間のつくり方を束縛するものではありません。私は機能主義者ではないのです。しかし、どんな空間であれ、計画上あるいは設計上のいずれかの機能があります。ここでいう「機能」とは、部屋の存在論的な本質に関係するものです。「なぜ部屋はこのようなつくりになっていて、ほかであってはいけないのか」という追求です。私は部屋の性質よりも、この問いをずっと重視しています。

GH　確かにあなたはどの作品においても、建築的な追求をしていることが明確に窺えます。また、そうした追求が空間に独特の緊張感を与えていますね。先ほどから私が話している神殿については、あなたはどのように見ているのでしょうか。

VO　「神殿」という言葉を自分の建物に対して使いたくありません。しかしながら、神殿には参照性がないということには興味があります。なにも参照していないことと抽象概念というものの違いについて、過去の建築——それはある部分において私が建築家として目標とするところでもありますが——を例にとって説明しましょう。カンボジアのアンコールワットの寺院[fig.9]は抽象概念ですが、グアテマ

fig.9 アンコール・ワット（12世紀前半）
Angkor Wat, early 12th century

ラのティカルの神殿[fig.10]は発明であり、なにも参照していない建築です。抽象概念には起源や系譜がありますが、発明にはその前身となるものがありません。内容だけでなく、特性においてもなにも参照していないものを、私は発明と呼んでいます。抽象概念とはすべて、なにかの原点から変化し、さらに分岐したものです。アンコール・ワットは仏教の基礎となっているシャーマニズム信仰を表わしたもので、神々の座である須弥山とヒマラヤの山々がテーマとなっています。アンコール・ワットとは、そのような抽象概念を描写しているのです。寺院が山のように見えるのは、建造にあたった人々が自然を抽象的に描写したからなのです。一方、マヤの人々は神殿を建造するにあたってなにも描写していません。ティカルの神殿のあの形が、どのようにしてできたのかはまったく知られていません。外観上の原点となるものを、神殿の痕跡を辿っても見つけることができないのです。マヤの神殿は、マヤの人々の想像力による、純粋な発明なのです。抽象的ではない人工物をつくることのできる社会に、私はとても魅了されます。ギリシアの神殿は家の抽象化であり、ドーム型の構造物は天国の抽象化であり、アジアの寺院は山の抽象化ですが、コロンブスが到来する以前のマヤの神殿は、人々の想像を知的に投影したものです。私はマヤの人々のような仕事をしたいので、この両者の違いは非常に重要です。私は根本的に新しいなにか、発明と呼べるなにかをつくりたいと思っています。オリジナルのない、つまりなにも参照していない建築を目指しているのです。

GH　なにも参照していない建築というのは、純粋な建築という意味でしょうか。

Valerio Olgiati

fig.10 ティカル遺跡（紀元前3–10世紀）
Tikal Temple, 3rd century BCE - 10th century CE

VO　なんらかの信念を参照したり外的な議論を経ることなしに、独自に存在できる建築という意味です。おっしゃるとおり、純粋な建築といってもいいでしょう。

建築的に教え、考える

GH　あなたはメンドリシオ建築アカデミーで11年間、教鞭をとられています。あなたの教育観とはどのようなものなのでしょうか。また、事務所で設計の実務をすることと大学で教えることになんらかの関係性はありますか？

VO　大学では私は中立的です。大学はリラックスできる場所でもあります。

GH　リラックスですか。

VO　はい。というのは、事務所で建築について考えることはつねに闘いで、戦略的である必要があります。大学ではより気楽に建築に接することができます。闘うことは重要ではありません。戦略や戦術なしで、より自由に遊べるのです。また非常に重要なのは、自分の言いたいことを言えるということです。事務所でも言いたいことは言えますが、やりたいことをなんでもやれるわけではありません。教えることはセラピーや休日のようなもので、とても楽しいです。特に素晴らしいと感じ

るのは、メンドリシオには世界中から学生が集まっているという点です。さまざまなアイデアとバックグラウンドを持っている学生たちが好きで、彼らと一緒にいると、世界をより深く理解することができます。

GH　なるほど。では今日における建築教育の意味についてはどのように考えていますか。

VO　私には、本質的な建築学がなぜ大学で完全に無視されているのかがわかりません。私は芸術、数学、社会学など、ほかの学問分野から手法や仕組みを取り込むことには興味がありません。また、そうした建築に付随する手法がたどる複雑な形態を建築に再度適用することにも関心はありません。言ってしまえば、私は非論理的なのです。建築が革新的でないとか、境界を広げられないということではないんです。しかし、付随する内容や手法といったものから、建築の拡張がもたらされることはないでしょう。自らの境界を打ち破ることができる建築にこそ真の成長があると確信しています。なぜ多くの建築家たちが、建築を生みだすために建築の外の領域で奮闘しているのか、私には不思議でなりません。

　驚くべきことに、建築教育においても、現象的な考察が重視されています。すべての現象的なアプローチは建築外のことがベースになっていて、建築学を豊かにしたり再構築したりするものでなく、短命なトレンドにすぎません。私は、建築の現象的な側面を否定するわけではありません。現象的な側面が建築の一部であることは確かですが、建築をかたちづくるすべての過程が現象的アプローチの影響下にある必要などないのです。建築を現象的に見ている建築家は、じつはその時点ですでに失格で、現象を本質的に取り扱う必要がある現象学的アプローチをとれていない、というのは疑った見方でしょうか？　そのような信条を建築家が表明すること自体、現象学的態度になくてはならない文化的な純粋さがすでに合理的な思考に置き換えられてしまっていることの証左です。現象的なアプローチには、ミニマルアートと同様の問題があります。ミニマルアートにおいても、参照となるものを描写しないことが重要です。繰り返しますが、このような建築に付随する歪んだ構造のすべてが、建築にとって意味のないことなのです。例として挙げるのは建築に付随するほかの影響でもよかったのですが、私がミニマリストを選んで現象的アプローチを関連づけたのは、私の建築が「ミニマリズム」と解釈されることがあるからかもしれません。これは完全に誤った解釈なのです。私は建築的に隅々まで考え抜いています。建築学的に考えることは特別に豊かなことで、とても楽しいことです。実際のところ、私が目指しているのは、なんの参照性も持たないやり方で建築

を拡張していくことです。つまり、純粋な建築を夢見ているのです！

GH　プロジェクトの設計段階においてアイデアがしっくりくる瞬間はどのようなときですか？

VO　そのような感覚に対する問いは、時代性や住んでいる場所の文化に完全に依存しています。感覚に対する問いは、欧米諸国よりもアジア諸国で重要視されているでしょう。すでに言ったとおり、そうした問いは個人もしくは社会的解釈によるものなので、私には興味がありません。しかし、建築に対する取り組み方として、根本的に違う方法があると考えています。この違いによって、建築の理解のされ方に違いが出てくると言えるかもしれません。私は基本的に、建築家には組立者（assembler）と分解者（divider）の2種類があると思っています。私自身は分解者でしょう。組立者——あるいは構成者（composer）と言ってもいいかもしれませんが——は、より動物的で、それほど精神的努力をせずに仕事をこなします。一方で、分解者はより複雑な業務に取り組み、戦略的に動いて目標を設定します。分解者の建築は特定の普遍的な形から出発しますが、それらは主にアイデアを反映させたものです。分解者は構造物として存在できるようになるまで、アイデアを分割するのです。アイデアから始めたら、構造から空間まで、機能から表現まで、すべてを完全に適合させなくてはいけません。そういった過程を経ながら、ひとつのものをデザインするということが最も困難な仕事なのです。

1——ルドルフ・オルジャティ（1910-95）：スイス出身の建築家。スイスの山里フリムスで数多くの住宅や施設を設計した。
2——坂本一成（1943-）：日本の建築家。1991年から2009年まで東京工業大学教授。主な建築に《散田の家》(1969)、《コモンシティ星田》(1992)、《House SA》(1999)がある。

対話を終えて ｜ After the conversation

　ヴァレリオ・オルジャティはスイスのフリムスに拠点を置いて活動し、国際的な人気を誇る建築家である。

　対話のなかで彼は「根本的に新しいなにか、発明と呼べるなにかをつくりたい」とはっきりと語った。振り返ってみると今回の6組の建築家のなかで建築の「新しさ」や「発明」を強調したのは彼だけだが、彼の思考のあり方、そして彼の作品は、見た目の新しさを表現するものではない。見た目が古いか新しいかを問う以前の、根源的な問いをわれわれに投げかける建築をつくろうとする。自分の建築が人々の「思考を刺激する」ことを重視するという言葉のとおり、彼が希求する「新しさ」とは、建築と人間の関係を根源的に捉え直すことだ。あるいは部屋の性質そのものよりも、「その部屋はそれ以外のつくりではいけないのか」という存在論的な本質を追求することだ。こうした彼の指向を受けて、僕は彼の建築に宿る「神殿性」を指摘した。彼はそれをやんわりと退ける一方で、神殿が「コンテクストに依らない」あるいは「参照性がない」ことへの共感を語り、そのことがたいへん興味深かった。

　彼は教師としても有名である。2002年より教鞭をとっているメンドリシオ建築アカデミーにおいて、オルジャティのアトリエはいつも独特な雰囲気で満たされている。各セメスターごとに3つのキーワード（例えば「白」「重さ」「公共空間」）が提示され、学生はそのキーワードをもとにプロジェクトをつくる。敷地やプログラムは各自で決める。ほかのアトリエと比べるときわめて自由だ。オルジャティが学生に求めているのは敷地やプログラムを上手く解くことではなく、建築的なアイデアを立ち上げそれを徹底的に思考することなのだ。「建築的に教え、考えたい」という彼

Valerio Olgiati is an architect based in Flims, Switzerland, who enjoys a popularity that is global in scale.

In our conversation he declared unequivocally that "I would like to make something that is radically new, something that is invented." In hindsight, he was the only one of the six architects or architect teams I interviewed for this book who prioritized "newness" and "invention" in architecture. Yet neither his philosophy nor his works express newness in the superficially visual sense. Rather, he aims to create architecture that challenges us with more fundamental questions than that of whether a building appears "old" or "new." In his own words, what is important to him is that his "architecture stimulates thought." The newness he seeks is in a basic rethinking of the relationship between architecture and people. Rather than the characteristics of a room, for example, he is concerned with what he calls its ontological foundation, "a quest to find out why a room should be one specific way and no other." My reaction to his approach prompted me to describe his buildings as "temple-like," an impression that he gently but firmly rejected. But he went on to speak of the affinity he feels for the "non-contextuality" or "non-referentiality" of temples, a point I found tremendously intriguing.

Olgiati is also famous as a teacher. At the Accademy of Architecture in Mendrisio, where he has taught since 2002, his atelier is always filled with a distinctive atmosphere. Every semester he presents three keywords (for example: white, weight, public space) on the basis of which his students develop projects, and it is up to them to choose the site and the program for

のもとで学生たちは奮闘する。

　最後に、昨夏訪れた彼の最新作であるポルトガルの自邸《ヴィラ・アレム》(2014)について少しだけ書きたい。およそ住宅とは思えないコンクリート造の巨大な建築物が荒野のなかに建っていた。ちょうど蓋を開けた箱のように、4方向に斜め上に突き出された庇がさまざまなイメージをかきたてる。プランの約4分の3は中庭。残り約4分の1の室内には、プランからは想像できないとても多様で豊かな体験が展開する。特にまったく別世界の2つのゾーン(リビングとベッドルーム群)を繋げるU字型の暗闇の廊下の体験はスリリングでとても新鮮だった。彼の代表作になるであろうこの自邸は、まさに「なにも参照していない建築」を謳いあげているかのようだった。

their project. Compared to other ateliers, it is an extremely free environment. What Olgiati demands of his students is not a clever choice of site or program, but the creation and thorough contemplation of architectural ideas. The students are challenged to respond to a teacher who strives to "teach and think architectonically."

　In closing I'd like to say something about his most recent work, the Villa Além (2014), his own residence in Portugal, which I visited last summer. A massive concrete structure that hardly resembled a house stood in the midst of a wilderness. Like a box whose top flaps had just been opened, its eaves thrust up and out obliquely in four directions, evoking all sorts of images. About three-quarters of the plan consists of an inner courtyard. The rooms that occupy the remaining quarter offer a rich diversity of experiences that the plan gives no hint of. Most novel and thrilling for me was the sensation of the dark, U-shaped corridor that connects the two utterly distinct zones of the living area and bedrooms. This house of his, which epitomizes the freedom of "architecture without references," will surely become known as one of his most representative works.

パスペルスの小学校／スイス／1998
School in Paspels/Switzerland/1998

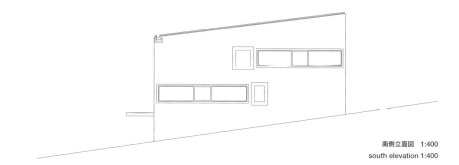

南側立面図 1:400
south elevation 1:400

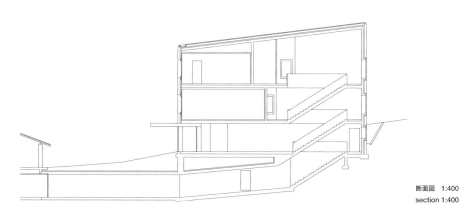

断面図 1:400
section 1:400

Valerio Olgiati

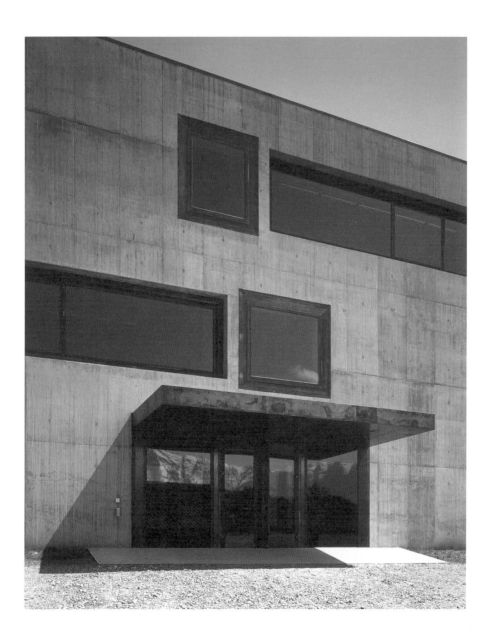

Valerio Olgiati

パスペルスの小学校
School in Paspels

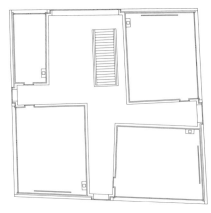

2階平面図　1:400
second floor plan 1:400

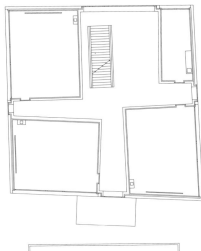

1階平面図　1:400
first floor plan 1:400

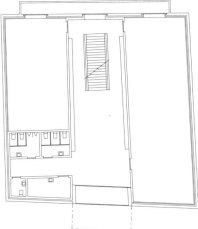

地下1階平面図　1:400
basement floor plan 1:400

Valerio Olgiati

Valerio Olgiati

パスペルスの小学校
School in Paspels

Valerio Olgiati

Valerio Olgiati

Valerio Olgiati

Atelier Bardill / Scharans, Switzerland / 2007

Valerio Olgiati

リナード・バルディルのアトリエ
Atelier Bardill

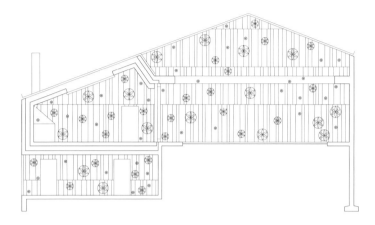

断面図　1:200
section 1:200

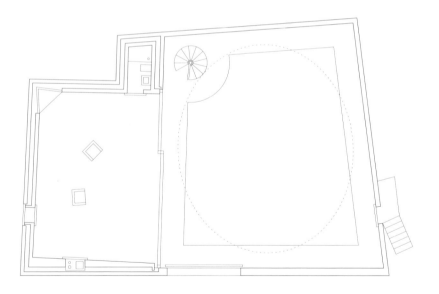

1階平面図　1:200
first floor plan 1:200

Valerio Olgiati

Valerio Olgiati

Peter Märkli

20th December 2013
@ Atelier in Hardstrasse, Zürich, Switzerland

Peter Märkli

History in contemporary architecture

Go Hasegawa   I can find an original and special sense of history in your works. That's why I would like to start with this question: What do you think about the meaning of history for contemporary architecture?

Peter Märkli   Your question is a central topic and we could talk until next week about it. We didn't grow up in the same context, so it's best if I explain to you how I started. I always wanted to become an architect. Besides the university, I was inspired by two elder personalities, Rudolf Olgiati and Hans Josephsohn[1]. That was my world.

For example, I discussed the column with Rudolf Olgiati. He would build a dark intermediate space as support between the column shaft and the horizontal element, because he couldn't use the capital, which was a tragedy. Because of the darkness, the horizontal element is floating above the column and therefore doesn't represent the vertical load. Normally this was done with the element of the capital by making it a sculpture with shadows or with leaves, and leaves do not carry load. They never show heaviness, but dematerialization. This was an elementary experience and an elementary question for me. When I understood this—and "understanding" means insight, not knowledge—I gained my first sense of certainty about my profession.

At Swiss Federal Institute of Technology Zürich (ETH Zürich), I would attend lectures about Mies van der Rohe and Le Corbusier, but I needed to start much earlier in history. And I needed to discover the world step by step, in order to understand the works by Mies or Le Corbusier. We all have a heritage and history in us. When we educate ourselves, we certainly need to know the past.

But when a person works artistically, there is no chronological order of the past, only interests. This means that when I work, I choose things in a subjective way, what touches me. And there are various pasts. There are younger and older pasts, but they always remain pasts. Our professors still saw Modernism as a motivation to continue working. It was still up-to-date for them. For me as a young student, Modernism was a past like Renaissance, Roman, or early Greek buildings.

GH   I see. As an architect what do you think about history concretely?

PM   When I talk to young students, we don't talk about whether something is beautiful or not, but why it has this appearance and why this form was chosen. There are classical examples from architecture with architects as authors, but also many secular examples. And in order to show how it has influenced me, I include some personal works by me.

I found images of my early work Two-Family House in Merls (1982) which were taken by someone, and it interested me a lot. It was influenced by a Romanesque church in Tuscania, Italy, San Pietro (c. 1000), and there are elements from the influence of Rudolf Olgiati. Here, there is more space between the columns and the horizontal supports. Then, ten years ago, I visited a villa by Palladio in the countryside, the Villa Valmarana in Vigardolo (1541-43). I walked around a corner and discovered this façade. I didn't know it before, but then I remembered the two-family house I had built, which looks the same [fig.1]. That is exactly the treasure of history.

This really meant a lot to me and I would say these people from the Renaissance, who turned themselves toward the ancient world, were influenced by certain buildings from antiquity, but at the same time they also spent their everyday life in these surroundings. So they were not only influenced by certain buildings they were looking at, but also by things, which are permanently around you, consciously or perhaps unconsciously.

GH   It's interesting that you talk about unconscious influences.

Then, what do you think about new things? For example, new technologies have changed our way of living. Le Corbusier wrote about cars and machines in *Vers une Architecture* (1923) — the new technologies of that period. He was conscious of new life in his era.

PM   Yes, but I don't agree with that. I think he lived in a period when people didn't recognize the beauty in technical products. For me, it was rather a didactic thing. He saw the aesthetic aspect of technical products and at the same time he was influenced by simple farmhouses in Switzerland, with their strip windows, and certainly he knew the whole history. These machines at the beginning of the 20th century were a vision of life, a motif for work and something to admire.

We do not have the same relation to machines anymore, because we were born a hundred years later. For us it's a deep past, which we need to look at critically.

By the way, there are big pillars by Le Corbusier at the Swiss Pavilion in Paris (1931). Why did he do such a thing? How did he come to this expression? I assume that he saw the bundled columns of Palazzo Chiericati in Vicenza by Palladio, and created his own pillars from it. That was his inspiration.

I just ask myself, what does it mean to us if they can fly to the moon? The only difference in buildings between the Renaissance and today, for example, is that we have more comfort. I think it is an illusion to believe that various media can change people fundamentally. I stick to an understanding of human beings as they have existed until now, more or less independently of all new developments and discoveries.

GH   Do you often refer to the Renaissance?

PM   When I was young, I once saw a movie about Mies van der Rohe. After seeing it, everything inside me fell apart in emptiness, because his work had impressed me so much. But after a night's sleep, I stepped out into the street in the morning and then everything came back again and I recognized that there are still many questions to answer and many things to do. As you know, the architectural language of Mies is reduced to a minimum, so that it is not possible to develop it any further. It's also not possible to add something to it. But the architecture of the Renaissance and Palladio can be developed further.

GH   Palladio rather than Mies. It's interesting and I agree now it's time to re-think about the Renaissance.

Expressions of our time

GH   I visited your recent project, the Neubau Synthes (2012) [fig.2]. I got the impression you paid much attention to the pillars on the façade.

PM   Solothurn is a very beautiful Baroque city and we planned our building in relation to the city in the sense of urban planning, but not in the formal aspect. The expression and appearance are my personal choice.

——   Peter Märkli refers to three images pinned on the wall [fig.3].

PM   In "Baukunst" (architecture) there is always the aspect of economy. These examples are the Palazzo Thiene Bonin Longare in Vicenza built by Vincenzo Scamozzi, and the Palazzo Rucellai in Florence. In the Palazzo Thiene Bonin Longare, we see the column, the capital, the horizontal element, and the base.

And in the Palazzo Rucellai are the same elements with a pilaster[2]. What interested me was to combine these two elements as a knot at the crossing point, without the base and the capital, and to place it on the level of the horizontal element. This creates for the eyes an effect like that of single independent elements, and it is kind of a summary of them.

GH   The difference between these buildings lies also in the possibilities of the technology of the time. Some proportions of your building are possible only today through the use of precast concrete elements, a modern technology.

PM   Yes, of course. The combination of and relation between the precast concrete and the stone, for example. A certain reference is made with the stone, but a lot of new things are added to it as well. Everything together is our appearance. It is a translation to a new and fresh appearance and expression, but it is also a matter of economy, the economy of "Baukunst." This amount of expensive stone is just enough to clarify and express the urbanistic relation to the old Baroque city. And the precast concrete elements cost less than concrete elements with stone cladding. This can be learned from the past. They used massive stone for the base and capital, but the column was made of brick and plaster, because it was cheaper. And the column was the most elaborate and expensive element in architecture. When a church was built and stone columns were fabricated in Egypt or somewhere, it was very expensive. A pilaster would cost much less than a column fabricated somewhere. At the Basilica San Marco in Venice, the columns all come from different countries, which were defeated in war.

As you suggested, it is only possible to build like this today—without pillars in a huge space of 600 square meters. It is only possible with precast concrete elements, which means that it is absolutely a building of our time. And the basic structure has to do with urban planning as well.

GH   What did you think about the meaning of these thin pillars?

PM   The whole building has a depth of 32 meters. In order to create interesting spaces for the people working inside, the façade is treated spatially. The external and internal façades on their own are not enough and therefore they can only compose the façade together. These two appearances together create the façade. The proportions of the external façade represent the large space of the landscape, while the proportions of the internal façade represent the relation between the floors and the working spaces, and are reduced to the scale of human beings.

GH   I see. The pillars were for the arrangement of different scales between the landscape and working spaces.

"Building culture" and synthesis

GH   To me it looks like you started with your Novartis Campus Visitor Center (2006) [fig.4] to use materials differently compared with the houses in the beginning. It seems you are positive about using different materials now, as in the Synthes office building.

PM   Yes, because I have more experience with materials now. I also learned a lot from paintings.

—— Peter Märkli shows an image of a painting by Henri Matisse[3].

PM   We can recognize a very simple construct of space in this painting by Henri Matisse ("The Painter and His Model," 1916-17) [fig.5]. Matisse then does something incredible. The wall is black and the floor as well. The black and white colors complete the painting independently from the construct of space, just like that! I looked at this painting various times and suddenly I understood it. That's why the stone is used as floor and wall at the same time, or also differently in the Visitor Center and Synthes. I use four different materials, but they are not the ceiling, wall or floor. I use the materials independently from the ceiling, wall and floor, and this creates a new and fresh appearance. In the building in Solothurn, this was applied explicitly.

The rough plaster with pebbles appears outside and inside, and we only used half of the usual material so the gray base color would shine through the rough plaster, which isn't completely covering it. The plaster receives a different appearance. The contractor actually disliked this plaster, but I find it beautiful. We had to fight for it. I thought it looked like Jackson Pollock[4], an "all-over painting."

GH   Since the Novartis Campus Visitor Center, do you think you have changed a bit from the beginning of your work?

PM   Yes, that's true. But actually it's always the case. My personality doesn't change, though. The interest in the profession is a process as well and every year we see something, perhaps a few new things. But the person who does the work remains the same. It's like when you look at the paintings of Cézanne[5] or the work of Sigurd Lewerentz[6] — the young, the middle-aged and the old.

Also we are interested in the questions of our profession, and this is the reason why the work will always look different from that of previous history. People of the early Greek period, for example, only knew the flat reliefs of Egypt, and it took a long time until they discovered the plastic relief for the metope[7] of the Greek temple. But we can always look back, and it is a phenomenon of our time that things can be resolved in a shorter time by a single person today.

There are constantly new questions arising in much shorter time periods today—for example, concerning technology or how buildings should be insulated. They didn't insulate buildings for hundreds of years. In the seventies they began to insulate buildings and today the thermal insulation is very thick. We need answers in short intervals to new questions. Lifestyles change quickly as well.

When you look at our "building culture," it is not only created by single works of magnificent architects. All people participate in it. Culture is something in which everyone participates. All these people had culture, and without any architects great buildings were made. We also have these magnificent palazzi in Rome. When I walk down the street, I get something from these buildings without entering them.

GH   That's true.

PM   But today the expression of pleasure, money and freedom is made by cars, travel, and having four toilets in the house. Now what does a Russian oligarch like Roman Abramovich[8] do? He doesn't build a palazzo, but instead he has a yacht somewhere in the ocean. Should I go past it? There is no contribution to culture from all this money, because it is all privatized. And culture is something everyone can be a part of, whether people have some money, a lot or a little. Of course they don't need to own it, but we also get something today from Venice, which invested its fortune in buildings that we can admire even today.

GH   Do you think it's possible that architecture will change our society?

PM   Not directly. Architecture surely influences people, but when there is a renewal of society, it never arises from the profession of the visual arts. It is always sociopolitical, economic, and other factors that create conditions to make certain developments subsequently possible. Good and beautiful environments civilize people for sure, but dreadful things happen in beautiful environments as well. I don't believe very much in these kinds of things. Nevertheless, it is important that we insist on keeping the environment intact.

GH   "Building culture" is a very interesting topic. Now I remember. When I was a student, I visited the sculpture museum in Giornico, La Congiunta (1992) [fig.6, 7]. I was very impressed by your building, and furthermore by the experience of the museum, which starts from the restaurant where you borrow the key.
Actually Giornico is a very beautiful village. Every house is made of stone and there is a small river, a nice landscape and a church. So it's not only the experience of seeing the sculptures of Josephsohn, but you designed the experience of the village as well.

PM   As you mention, there are the river, the stones, the bridges, the restaurant, the church, and a piece of landscape. Also thanks to the railroad, the vineyard and the river, this place is unobstructed, which is very rare today. And because it is a museum for sculptures, the entrance is not oriented toward the village. A supermarket would have its entrance toward the village. In this way, one needs to make a movement through the space and turn in order to reach the entrance. It was our aim to integrate it with the village, and because there are none of the things there that we usually encounter in a museum, somebody needed to have the keys. And this could only be at the bar in the village, and also because people would sometimes eat or drink there.

GH   (laughs) So they were pleased with it?

PM   Yes, it's a synthesis. But also in France and Italy there are some remote churches where you need to ask for the key. A certain woman or family would have the key, otherwise you wouldn't be able to finance it at all. In Giornico, a man from the village also takes care of the surroundings and another man does the vineyards.

GH   This project is a very good example of how one building can reconfigure its environment, including the surrounding landscape and the people who live there.

Conveying experience

—— Peter Märkli shows some small sketches.

PM   First I make small sketches or small models like these. Later I make these big drawings [fig.8, 9].

GH   Do you make the models by yourself?

PM   Yes, I make them here in my atelier. But I don't make bigger models, because I like them without the details.

GH   So you basically like to think alone.

PM   Yes, it is necessary. I need to work with the drawings. My partners are the drawings. And when I know something more exactly, I talk with my collaborators. But not before, because I have to look first by myself. Also, I prefer to work here.

GH   So you never develop a project through discussion with your collaborators?

PM   No, I don't like that. It's clear that I like to discuss things with people, but when it needs to be precise, I first need to work by myself.

For me, the center of every artistic profession is the "idea." The idea is shown through a sketch, and therefore the sketch is the most valuable thing. An enormous amount of work is necessary in order to maintain something of the idea and the sketch in the final painting, sculpture or building, to keep this immediacy and freshness. I need to discuss each variation during the development of the project in order to give every element the right place. Every element has a meaning.

If you have many employees and you have a sketch, then when you enter the finished building, you realize that there was no attention given to the toilets, the underground levels or the parking spaces. I love to work through every element, and that's the reason I can employ only 15 people.

GH   You are famous as a teacher as well. You are teaching at ETH Zürich and you work in your office. Is there a relationship between the two?

PM   I think so. If you work with someone for a long time, they already know something. When I go to ETH Zürich and meet young students for the first time, I need to give broader explanations. But I don't think that I have an education for teaching. I can only speak to people about my profession and tell them: "You are architects, and I'm an architect. The only difference between you and me is the amount of experience in the profession." Therefore I can only speak to architects and not to students. And I try to pass on the experience that I have. It is a big task today to question general customs and habits. It is also a big effort for the students to develop a certain freedom of thinking, in order to see things and formulate them in a new way—to gain a new perception and not to do things as they have always been done.

Basically we are influenced by everything, and it's clear that we receive some input through teaching. You need to give a lot, and you can only teach well when you have something to give, when you are not tired and still have many inspirations. I think it's mostly in this direction and less the other way around. In the world of today, where everything is becoming uniform, we need to help young people discover themselves. It's important that they see and discover on their own, and take care of their sensitivity.

GH   This will be the last question. Your way of thinking as I heard it today was very interesting. What, then, is the "architectural" in architecture for you?

PM   What we try to express through architecture is a question, which concerns us not only as architects, but also primarily as a person. Before we are architects, we are individuals with a certain view toward life. For me, it is expressed through the dimensions of a building, which are numbers, and their relation to each other, the proportions.

GH   So when you are drawing sketches, you think a lot about the dimensions.

PM   In the sketches, all elements of the project are there. But the dimensions are expressed in simple drawings, which are drawn only with lines. Without any color, surface or shadow. So I make drawings of the building only with lines and the basic dimensions—the most important building dimensions, which are the outer dimensions. Then the dimensions of the ceiling height and of the windows can be added later.

GH   So for you, "architectural" means the dimensions of a building?

PM   Yes, through the dimensions of a building, the "architectural" element is fixed and determined.

1 —— Hans Josephsohn: Born in 1920, deceased in 2012. A sculptor originally from then-Eastern Prussia who worked extensively in Switzerland. He is known for sculptural works based on motifs from parts of human anatomy, such as plaster busts and reclining figures.

2 —— The base: The lowest part of a column, consists of multiple, vertically stacked mouldings. Doric columns have no base, while Ionic, Corinthian and other columns have distinct base designs that vary with the order.

3 —— Pilaster: A form of decorative column that is integrated into wall surfaces. In the Palazzo Rucellai, pilasters are articulated on every level, thereby striating the external appearance.

4 —— Henri Matisse: French artist born in 1869 and deceased in 1954. Known as a leading artist of Fauvism, he pursued an aesthetic world saturated with a unique sense of colors. Masterpieces include "Dance (I)" (1909).

5 —— Jackson Pollock: American artist of the abstract expressionism movement, born in 1912 and deceased in 1956. Beginning with action painting that engendered chaotic and dynamic expressions, he masterfully deployed techniques such as all-over, dripping, and pouring to attain balance within chaotic compositions.

6 —— Paul Cézanne: French artist born in 1839 and deceased in 1906. Though considered to be a member of the Impressionist movement in the beginning, he increasingly began to pursue formalism embodied in still-life and landscapes. Masterpieces include "Mont Sainte-Victoire Seen from Bellevue" (c. 1885).

7 —— Sigurd Lewerentz: Swedish architect born in 1885 and deceased in 1975. He designed Skogskyrkogården (The Wooden Cemetery) (1940) in collaboration with Gunnar Asplund, and Markuskyrkan (Church of Saint Mark) (1963).

8 —— Metope: An architectural element installed in the entablature, below the pediment in classical temple architecture.

9 —— Roman Abramovich: Russian entrepreneur born in 1966. Multi-billionaire who is also the owner of a British soccer team.

ペーター・メルクリ

2013年12月20日
スイス、チューリッヒ、ハルト通りのアトリエにて

現代建築にとっての歴史

長谷川豪(以下、GH) あなたの建築作品には、その背景に特別な歴史観があることが感じられます。まずは歴史についての話から伺いたいのですが、いま現代建築にとって歴史はどのような意味を持つと考えられていますか。

ペーター・メルクリ(以下、PM) あなたの質問はとても重要な話題で、1週間でもずっと話していられるテーマですね。しかし私たちの文化的なバックグラウンドは異なりますから、最初に、私がこの仕事をどのようにスタートさせたかをお話しするのがよいでしょう。私は建築家になりたいとずっと思っていました。大学時代を別にすれば、2人の先達から大きな影響を受けました。ルドルフ・オルジャティとハンス・ヨゼフソン[1]です。この2人が私の世界観に大きな影響を及ぼしたのです。

　例えば、ルドルフ・オルジャティとは柱について議論をしました。彼は柱体と水平要素のあいだを支持する部材として、暗い中間層をつくろうとしていました。彼は形骸化した柱頭を使おうとしなかったからです。彼の建築では中間層の影によって水平要素は柱の上に浮いて見え、垂直荷重を支えているようには見えません。通常は、この部分には柱頭が用いられ、そこに陰影のある彫刻あるいは葉模様を施していましたが、植物が荷重を支えることはありません。それらはけっして重量感の表現などではなく、脱物質化を表わしているのです。これは私にとって初歩的な経験であったとともに、初歩的な自問も起こりました。そして私がこの問いを理解したとき——ここでいう理解とは単なる知識ではなく本質を見抜くという意味ですが——はじめて、建築という自分が選んだ職業についての手応えを感じることがで

きました。

 スイス連邦工科大学チューリッヒ校（ETH Zürich）では、ミース・ファン・デル・ローエやル・コルビュジエに関する講義に出るつもりでしたが、まずはそれ以前の歴史について学ぶ必要がありました。ミースやル・コルビュジエの作品を理解するためには、世界について順を追って把握していく必要があったのです。誰にとっても、過去から受け継いできたものや歴史があります。そしてなにかを学ぶためには、過去の出来事を知る必要があるのです。しかしながら、人が芸術的な仕事に携わるときには、そこには歴史的な年代といった序列はなく、単に興味というものがあるだけです。私が仕事をするときには、きわめて主観的に心惹かれた物事を選択しています。また、一口に「過去」と言っても、比較的近い過去もあれば大昔のこともありますが、それらはつねに「過去」のこととして同じように扱われています。私たちが学生の頃、大学の教授たちはなお、モダニズムを必死で説いていたのです。モダニズムは当時の彼らにとって最新のものだったかもしれませんが、その頃の私にはすでに過去のものであり、その点ではルネサンスやローマ、初期のギリシア建築などと同じでした。

GH なるほど。ではあなたの建築と歴史の関係について具体的に訊かせていただけますか？

PM 若い学生たちとは、どれが美しいかといったことは話しません。でも、なぜこういう外観なのか、なぜこの様式が選ばれたのか、ということについては話題にします。建築家を作家とみなしていた古典的な建築もありますが、世俗的な例も多くあります。そのようなものによって私がどのような影響を受けたのか、これまでに手がけた作品を例にして紹介しましょう。

 私の初期の仕事《2つの個人住宅》（1982）を誰かが撮影した写真を見つけたのですが、これは非常に興味深いものでした。この建物はイタリアのロマネスク式教会であるトゥスカーニアの《サン・ピエトロ寺院》（1000頃）の影響を受けているのですが、先ほどお話ししたルドルフ・オルジャティから影響を受けた部分もあります。この建築では柱と水平の支持材のあいだに、広いスペースをとっているのです。10年前になりますが、田園地帯にあるアンドレア・パッラーディオ設計のヴィラ、ヴィガルドロの《ヴィラ・ヴァルマラーナ》（1541–43）を訪れたときのことです。近くを歩いていると、ヴィラのファサードが目に入りました。そのファサードを見て——以前にはわからなかったのですが——、このヴィラは自分が設計した《2つの個人住宅》とまったく同じような外観であることに気づいたのです [fig.1]。まさに歴史のな

fig.1 上から《2つの個人住宅》(1982)、トゥスカーニアの《サン・ピエトロ寺院》(1000頃)
ヴィガルドロの《ヴィラ・ヴァルマラーナ》(1541 – 43)
Two-Family House (1982), San Pietro in Tuscania (c. 1000),
Villa Valmarana in Vigardolo (1541-43)

かの宝と言えます。

　このことは私にとってじつに意味深いことです。ルネサンス時代の人々はいにしえの世界に関心を持っていましたし、いにしえの建造物から影響を受けていた面もあるでしょう。しかし同時に、彼らはそのような建造物に囲まれて生活もしていたのです。ルネサンス時代の人々は、彼らが注目した特定の建造物からだけではなく、ずっと変わらず存在してきた周りの物事からも、おそらく無意識に影響を受けていました。

GH　無意識に受ける影響というのは興味深いお話ですね。歴史における新しい物事についてはどのようにお考えですか。例えば、新しいテクノロジーは私たちの生活様式をどんどん変えていきます。ル・コルビュジエは『建築をめざして』(1923) のなかで、当時の新しいテクノロジーであった自動車と機械について記しています。彼は新しい生活様式というものを意識していました。

PM　ええ、確かにそうです。ですが、私の考えは違います。私は、人々が技術的な製品の美しさを認識していなかった時代に彼は生きていたのだと考えています。これは私にとって少し教訓めいた話なのです。彼は技術的な製品の美的な側面を認めていましたが、同時に、横長の窓があるスイスの簡素な農家からも影響を受けていました。そうです、彼は明らかに、すべての歴史を把握していたのです。20世紀初頭には、機械は生活の理想像であり、作品のモティーフであり、称賛すべきものでした。しかしそれから100年が経過し、私たちと機械の関係性は変わってしまったのです。ル・コルビュジエの時代は、私たちが批判的に見る必要のある遠い過去のこととなっています。

　ところで、パリの《スイス学生会館》(1931) のピロティで、ル・コルビュジエは大きな柱を用いています。なぜ彼はそんなことをしたのでしょうか。どのようにして、この表現方法を思いついたのでしょうか。パッラーディオのヴィチェンツァの《パラッツォ・キエリカーティ》(1548–57) の柱の連なりを見てひらめき、独自の柱のイメージをつくり上げたのではないかというのが私の考えです。

　試みに自問自答してみるのですが、もし月まで飛べるとしたら、私たちにとってそれはどんな意味があるでしょうか。例えば、ルネサンスと現代の建築の違いは、現代のほうがより快適だというだけです。人々がさまざまなメディアによって根本的に変わるというのは幻想でしょう。あらゆる新しい進歩や発見とは別に、私はこれまで存在してきた人間そのものの理解にこだわっているのです。

fig.2 シンセスの新施設（2012）
Neubau Synthes, 2012

GH　よくルネサンスを引き合いに出されますね。

PM　若い頃に一度、ミース・ファン・デル・ローエについての映画を観たのですが、彼の作品に強く感銘を受けすぎたため、むなしさがこみあげてきて、どうしていいかわからなくなりました。ところが、一晩寝てから街へ出かけると、元の感覚を取り戻し、解決すべき問題ややるべきことがまだたくさんあることに気づきました。ご存じのとおり、ミースの建築言語は最小限まで削られており、それ以上発展させることは不可能です。なにかを加えることもできません。しかし、ルネサンスやパッラーディオの建築は、さらに発展させることができるのです。

GH　ミースよりもパッラーディオだというのはとても興味深いことです。たしかにいま、ルネサンスを再考すべき時代状況だというのはよくわかります。

現代の表現

GH　あなたの最近のプロジェクトである《シンセスの新施設》(2012) [fig.2]を訪ねたのですが、ファサードの柱にとても配慮しているという印象を受けました。

PM　建物が建っているゾロトゥルンはとても美しいバロック様式の街です。私たちは都市計画という点でこの街と関係性のある建物を計画しましたが、堅苦しいも

fig.3 左からヴィチェンツァの《パラッツォ・ティエーネ・ボニン》(1572)、
フィレンツェの《パラッツォ・ルチェッライ》(1446 – 51)、《シンセスの新施設》
From left, Palazzo Thiene Bonin Longare in Vicenza (1572),
Palazzo Rucellai in Florence (1446-51), Neubau Synthes

のは避けました。表現と外観は、私の個人的な選択によるものです。

──── ペーター・メルクリ、壁の3枚の写真を指す [fig.3]

PM 「建築(Baukunst)」にはつねに経済的な問題がつきまといます。ヴィチェンツァにあるヴィツェンツォ・スカモッツィによって建てられた《パラッツォ・ティエーネ・ボニン》(1572)とフィレンツェの《パラッツォ・ルチェッライ》(1446–51)でも同様です。例えば《パラッツォ・ティエーネ・ボニン》には柱、柱頭、水平要素、そして柱礎[2]があります。そして《パラッツォ・ルチェッライ》には同じ要素のピラスター[3]があります。私が興味を持ったのは、柱礎も柱頭もなしで、水平要素と柱が交差する部分でこれら2つの要素を結び目として統合することでした。これによって、単独の独立した要素であるかのような錯覚を生みだしていると言えるでしょう。

GH 面白いですね。しかし同時に、これらの建物の違いは、それぞれの時代のテクノロジーにも起因しています。あなたが手がけた建物は、現代のテクノロジーであるプレキャスト・コンクリートによる、この時代でなければ不可能なプロポーションの建築だと言うこともできませんか。

PM ええ、もちろんです。プレキャスト・コンクリートと石材の組み合わせや、

その関係性などを例に挙げることができるでしょう。ある部分は石材と関係していますが、同じように多くの新しいことも取り入れています。《シンセスの新施設》ではすべてが同時に存在しています。そしてそのことが新鮮な表出、表現となっていくのですが、それは同時に経済的、「建築」の経済的な問題とも関係しています。これだけの量の高価な石材を用いることで、かろうじて、古いバロック様式の街との都市的な関係性を明確に表現できるのです。プレキャスト・コンクリートであれば、石材で被覆したコンクリートより低コストで済みます。こういったことは、過去からも明らかなのです。昔の人々は柱礎と柱頭に大量の石材を使っていましたが、柱にはれんがや漆喰を用いていました。そうするほうが経済的だからです。かつて柱は建築において最も繊細で高価な要素でした。教会建設のための石柱はエジプトなどで加工されており、非常に高価だったのです。そうやって加工された柱よりも、漆喰はずっと安上がりでした。ヴェネツィアの《サン・マルコ寺院》(1063–73頃)で使われている柱はすべて、戦争に敗れたさまざまな国々から運び込まれています。

あなたが言うように、600m^{2}もの広さを持ちながら柱がないような空間は、現代でのみ可能です。それはプレキャスト・コンクリートを使った場合にのみに可能であり、間違いなくいまの時代の建物だと言えます。そしてこの建物の基本構造は都市計画と関係があるのです。

GH 《シンセスの新社屋》の細い柱の意味については、どうお考えですか。

PM 建物の全体的な奥行きは32mです。建物内で働く人たちにとって興味を惹くようなスペースにするために、ファサードを立面ではなく、空間として扱っています。外側と内側のファサードが個別に存在しているだけでは十分ではなく、それらが一緒になってこそ、このファサードを構成できるのです。ここでは外側と内側、2つのあらわれが一体となってファサードをつくり上げています。外ファサードのプロポーションはランドスケープのなかの大きな空間を表わしている一方で、内ファサードのプロポーションはフロアとワーキング・スペースの関係性を表現しており、ヒューマン・スケールに縮小されています。

GH なるほど。この2列の柱はランドスケープとワーキング・スペースという、異なるスケールに応答するためのものなのですね。

fig.4 ノバルティス・キャンパス・ビジターセンター（2006）
Novartis Campus Visitor Center, 2006

「建物文化」と総合的な経験

GH 《ノバルティス・キャンパス・ビジターセンター》(2006) [fig.4]では、初期の住宅とは異なった方法で素材が使われているように見えます。《シンセスの新施設》と同様に、最近はさまざまな素材を積極的に使われているようですね。

PM ええ、素材についてこれまで多くの経験を積みましたから。それから、絵画からも多くのことを学びました。

―― ペーター・メルクリ、アンリ・マティス[4]の絵の写真を見せる

PM このマティスの絵では、空間のコントラストは非常にシンプルです（《画家とそのモデル》1916-17) [fig.5]。ここでマティスは驚くべきことをしています。壁も床も黒色なのです。黒と白の色彩を空間の構図から独立させる、ただそれだけのことでこの絵は完成しているのです！　この絵を何度も見ていて、そのことを突然理解したのです。だから《ノバルティス・キャンパス・ビジターセンター》と《シンセスの新施設》では、石材を床と壁に同時に、あるいは違ったかたちで使いました。私は4つの異なる素材を使っていますが、天井や壁、床として使うのではありません。こういった素材を、天井や壁、床から独立して使うことで、新しく新鮮なあらわれとなるのです。《シンセスの新施設》には、この手法が明確に適用されています。

fig.5　アンリ・マティス《画家とそのモデル》(1916-17)
Henri Matisse, *The Painter and His Model*, 1916-17

　この建物では小石の混じった粗い漆喰を内外に使っています。漆喰は通常の半分ほどの量に抑えているため、その粗さによって灰色の地の部分が輝いて見えるでしょう。建物を完全に上塗りしているわけではないのです。この漆喰はあらわれに変化を与えてくれます。じつは施工業者はこの漆喰を嫌っていましたが、私は美しいと思っていましたので、漆喰をめぐって彼らと議論を戦わせました。私にはこの漆喰がジャクソン・ポロック[5]の「オールオーバー・ペインティング」のように見えます。

GH　《ノバルティス・キャンパス・ビジターセンター》以降、作風が少し変わったと、ご自身では思われますか？

PM　ええ、思います。私自身は変わりませんが、作風というものは変わり続けているのです。仕事における関心事もプロセスとして影響しますし、それ以外でも、同じ人物であっても、毎年なんらかの新しい出会いや発見で変化しているのです。例えばポール・セザンヌ[6]の絵やシーグルド・レヴェレンツ[7]の建築が、彼らが若い頃から歳をとるにつれ、変化していくのと同じです。

　それから、私たちが仕事にしている建築特有の問題もあります。技術の進歩があるので、作品は過去のものとはつねに異なったものになっていくでしょう。例えば、初期ギリシア時代の人々はエジプトの平面的なレリーフだけしか知らず、ギリシア神殿の柱上のメトープ[8]に用いられるような塑造による立体的なレリーフ

に到達するまで長い時間がかかりました。しかし、私たちはつねに過去から学ぶことができるし、現代では、ひとりの人間が短時間で問題を解決できるようになっています。

現代では、新しい問題が次々に生じます。例えばテクノロジーに関する問題であったり、建築物はどのように断熱されるべきか、といった問題です。建築物は何百年も前から断熱されてきたわけではありません。1970年代に断熱されはじめて以降、現代の断熱材は非常に厚くなっています。新しい問題に対する答えが短期間で要求され、生活様式もまた激しく変化しています。

私たちの「建物文化」を見れば、そこにあるのは、優秀な建築家たちの作品だけではありません。すべての人々が文化にかかわっています。文化とは、すべての人がかかわるものなのです。すべての人々に文化があり、建築家なしでも素晴らしい建築物が建てられてきました。ローマには素晴らしいパラッツォがあります。ローマの通りを歩けば、たとえそうした建物のなかに入らなくても、なにか得るものがあります。

GH　まったくそのとおりですね。

PM　しかし現代では、喜びやお金、自由といったものの表現手段が、自動車や旅行、あるいはトイレが4つもあるような住宅を持つことになってしまっています。ロマン・アブラモヴィッチ[9]のようなロシアの新興実業家はなにをしているのでしょうか。パラッツォを建てる代わりに、どこかの海に巨大ヨットを所有しています。これを見過ごすことができるでしょうか。こういったお金は、文化になにも貢献していません。すべてが個人的な物に費やされているからです。文化とは、お金をどの程度持っているかには関係なく、誰もがその一部となることができるものです。私たちはヴェネツィアの街を所有しているわけではありませんが、ヴェネツィアから得るものがあります。ヴェネツィアでは、現代でも賞賛に値するような建築物のために富を投資していたからです。

GH　そうですね。では建築によって、社会を刷新することは可能だと思われますか？

PM　直接的に変えることはできないでしょう。建築が人々に影響を与えることは確かですが、社会の刷新は、視覚芸術にかかわる職業からは起こりません。刷新はつねに政治社会学的、経済学的な要因から起こり、こういった要因によって発展が可能になります。良好で美しい環境は確実に文明化につながりますが、美しい環境

fig.6 彫刻の家(1992)
La Congiunta, 1992

Peter Märkli

であっても酷いことが起こりえます。私自身は、美しい環境で酷いことが起こるとはあまり考えていませんが。いずれにせよ、環境を保全し続けるよう主張することは重要です。

GH　さきほどの「建物文化」というのは、とても興味深いトピックです。私は学生の頃、ジョルニコの彫刻美術館《彫刻の家》(1992) [fig.6, 7]を訪れました。あなたが手がけられた建物はもちろん、レストランでカギを借りることから始まる美術館の体験に非常に感動しました。
　ジョルニコはじつに美しい村です。すべての家は石造りで、小川や素敵なランドスケープ、それから教会があります。ハンス・ヨゼフソンの彫刻を見るという体験だけでなく、村そのものを体験することも設計に取り込まれたのですね。

PM　そのとおりです。この村には、川、石、橋、レストラン、教会、ランドスケープがあります。鉄道とブドウ園、川といったもののおかげで、現代ではとても珍しく、見晴らしもいい場所です。もしもスーパーマーケットであれば建物の入口は村のほうを向いているでしょうが、これは彫刻を扱う美術館ですから、村のほうを向いてはいません。そのため、美術館の入口に辿り着くには、まわり道をする必要があります。美術館を村になじませることが私たちの狙いだったのです。通常の美術館とは大きく異なりますが、美術館のカギを誰かに預かってもらう必要がありました。これは、村のレストラン以外には考えられませんでした。美術館を訪れた人々が、このレストランで飲んだり食べたりすることもありますから。

GH　では、レストランのオーナーも喜んでいるんですね（笑）。

PM　ええ、これは総合的な経験です。ですが、フランスやイタリアにも、カギを借りないといけないような、人里離れた場所に教会があります。資金面での理由から、特定の女性や家族が教会のカギを持っているのです。ジョルニコでは、村の男性には、周辺の環境やブドウ園の管理といった仕事もありますから。

GH　このプロジェクトは、ひとつの建物によって、地域住民や周辺の景色も含めた環境が見事に再構築されている好例ですね。こうしたことも「建物文化」と言えそうです。

Peter Märkli

fig.7 彫刻の家
La Congiunta

Peter Märkli

fig.8 《ノバルティス・キャンパス・ビジターセンター》スケッチ
Novartis Campus Visitor Center, sketch

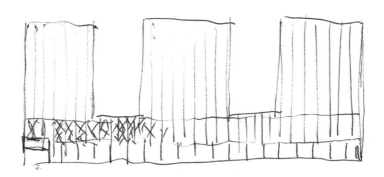

経験を伝えるということ

—— ペーター・メルクリ、小さなスケッチをいくつか見せる

PM　私の設計においては最初に、このような小さいスケッチを描いたり模型をつくったりします [fig.8, 9]。それから大きな図面に起こします。

GH　模型もありますが、これはご自身でつくられるのですか。

PM　ええ、模型はこのアトリエでつくります。しかし、大きな模型はつくりません。ディテールのない模型が好きなんです。

GH　基本的にひとりで考えるのがお好きなんですね。

PM　ええ、ひとりで考えることが必要です。スケッチを描かなければいけませんし、スケッチが私のパートナーです。状況をある程度把握できるようになってくれば、協同作業者と話をします。しかし、まずは自分で確認しなければなりません。それに、このアトリエで仕事をすることが好きなのです。

GH　では、協同作業者の方々と話し合いながら、プロジェクトを進めていくこと

fig.9 《ノバルティス・キャンパス・ビジターセンター》模型
Novartis Campus Visitor Center, model

はないのでしょうか。

PM　ええ、そういった方法は好きではないのです。人々と議論するのはもちろん好きですが、緻密さが必要なときはまず自分ひとりで作業しなければなりません。
　私にとって、あらゆる芸術的職業の中心にあるのは「アイデア」です。アイデアはスケッチを通して表現されますから、スケッチが最も貴重です。そのようなアイデアやスケッチの即時性や新鮮さを最終的な絵画、彫刻、建築でも保つためには、膨大な作業量が要求されます。プロジェクトを進めていくあいだには、あらゆる選択肢について検討し、すべてのエレメントが適切な場所におさまるようにする必要があります。すべてのエレメントには意味があるのです。
　もしも、多くのスタッフにスケッチを渡してあとは任せておくようなスタイルで進めていれば、実際に完成した建物では、トイレや地階、駐車場といった場所がなおざりになってしまうでしょう。私は、すべての部分できちんとした仕事がしたいのです。ですから、スタッフは15人しか雇えません。

GH　教育者としても有名でいらっしゃいますね。ETH Zürichで教鞭をとられていることと設計事務所でのお仕事に関連はありますか？

PM　関連していると思っています。長いあいだ一緒に仕事をしていれば、相手のことはよくわかっているでしょう。しかし、大学で若い学生たちと最初に会うとき

には、専門的な内容だけでなく、広範囲に及ぶ説明をする必要があります。私は、教え方について特別な教育を受けたとは考えていません。学生たちには、自分の職業である建築についての話ができるだけです。「あなたたちは建築家で、私も建築家です。違いは、職業上の経験の量だけです」と。つまりは、学生に対してではなく、建築家に対して話をするのです。私は自分の経験を伝えようとしています。常識や習慣についてあらためて考えるのは、現代では大変なことです。また、思考を自由にして、物事をどのように捉えて新しい方法に置き換えていくのか考えることも、学生にとっては簡単ではありません。しかし、そうやって新しい概念が得られ、従来と違う方法が身につくのです。

　基本的に、私たちはあらゆるものの影響を受けていますし、教えることを通してなんらかのインプットを得ているのも明らかです。しかし、教えるためには多くのことを提供する必要がありますし、提供できるものがあって疲れておらず、しかもひらめきが十分なときに、はじめて上手に教えることができるのです。教えるとはこのようになにかを提供しようと努力することがほとんどで、その逆はあまりないと私は思っています。すべてにおいて画一化されつつある現代の世界では、若者が自分を認識するための手助けが必要です。自分自身で物事を見て発見し、独自の感性を育むことが大事です。

GH　なるほど。今日のお話はとても心惹かれるものでした。最後に、あなたにとって「建築的であること」とはどういうことを意味しているかお訊かせくださいますか。

PM　建築を通じて私たちが表現しようとするものは問いです。それは建築家としてばかりでなく、まずはひとりの人間としての自分にかかわることです。私たちは建築家である前に、人生についてなんらかの考えを持った個人なのですから。私にとっては、それは建物の特性、つまり数字、相互の関係性、プロポーションによって表現されるものです。

GH　寸法について熟考されるのですね。

PM　スケッチにはプロジェクトのあらゆる要素が見て取れますが、正確な寸法というのは、線だけで描かれたシンプルな図面上に表わされます。色彩や面、陰影などのない図面です。だから私は、線と基本的な寸法だけのシンプルな図面を描くのです。最も重要な建物の寸法は、外側の寸法です。天井高や窓の寸法などは、後

で足していくことができます。

GH　では、「建築的」であるためには建物の寸法が最も重要だということですか？

PM　ええ、建物の寸法を通じて「建築的」なエレメントが決定されるのです。

1——ハンス・ヨゼフソン(1920-2012)：スイスで活躍した東プロイセン（当時）出身の彫刻家。石膏による胸像や横に寝そべる人物像など、人体の部位をモティーフとした彫刻作品で知られる。
2——柱礎：柱の土台用に複数の型を重ねてつくられた置き石。ドリス式には存在せず、イオニア式とコリント式ではそれぞれ造形が異なるなど、オーダーによって違いがある。
3——ピラスター：壁面と一体化した装飾柱で、付け柱とも呼ばれる。《パラッツォ・ルチェライ》では、ピラスターを階ごとに設けることで、外壁が層状に分節されている。
4——アンリ・マティス(1869-1954)：フランス出身の画家。野獣派(Fauvisme)の代表格として知られ、独特の色彩感覚あふれる世界観を追求した。代表作に《ダンスⅠ》(1909)がある。
5——ジャクソン・ポロック(1912-56)：アメリカ出身の抽象表現主義の画家。アクション・ペインティングによる無秩序で勢いのある表現や、オール・オーヴァーやドリッピング、ポーリングなどの技法により、混沌とした画のバランスを調整するための工夫が施されている。代表作に《秋のリズム》(1950)がある。
6——ポール・セザンヌ(1839-1906)：フランス出身の画家。初期は印象派のひとりとされていたが、やがて静物や風景に内在する造形性を探求するようになった。代表作に《サン・ヴィクトワール山》(1887頃)がある。
7——シーグルド・レヴェレンツ(1885-1975)：スウェーデン出身の建築家。グンナー・アスプルンドと共同での《森の葬祭場》(1940)や、《セント・マークス教会》(1963)を手がけた。
8——メトープ：神殿建築のエンタブラチュアにとりつけられた壁面部材。メトープにはしばしば彫刻による装飾が施されている。
9——ロマン・アブラモヴィッチ：ロシア出身の実業家(1966-)。イギリスのサッカー・チームのオーナーも務める大富豪。

対話を終えて | After the conversation

ペーター・メルクリのアトリエはチューリッヒの中心部から程近いブロックの中庭に建つ建物のなかにある。スタッフが働くオフィスは別の場所にあって、ここは彼がひとりでスケッチや模型をつくりプロジェクトを思考するための空間である。スケッチ、図面、模型、美術書のみのこざっぱりした部屋。壁にはハンス・ヨゼフソンの彫刻が掛けられている(p.102)。プライヴェートな雰囲気でほどよい緊張感があって、これほどアトリエらしいアトリエを訪れるのは初めてだ。彼は考える空間(アトリエ)／協同者と話し合い図面を描く空間(オフィス)の2つを分けてプロジェクトを構築することを大切にしている。

　メルクリは歴史について多くを語ってくれた。ミースの建築は発展不可能だが、ルネサンスやパッラーディオの建築はさらに発展させることが可能だとし、現代とルネサンスの建築の違いは現代の建築空間のほうがより快適だというだけ、とさえ言い切る。今日を書き換えさらにその先を表現しようとするモダニズム思考よりも、歴史上の建築がなぜそういう形になっているのかを設計者の意図や通説とは関係なく自ら遡って推測し、過去の豊かさを更新し続けるルネサンスの思考は現代でも可能だと説く。これが単なる保守ではないことはメルクリの作品を見れば明らかだろう。新しさというイデオロギーに絡めとられないで、現在と過去の豊かさを同時に耕すこと。コンセプトを明確に打ち出すモダニズムのようなわかりやすさは求めていない。「私はこれまで存在してきた人間そのものの理解にこだわっているのです」という言葉が強く印象に残った。

　また僕が対話のなかでも《彫刻の家》を例にして指摘したことだが、メルクリの作品は建築単体だけでなく、その建築が成立す

Peter Märkli's atelier is in a building that faces the inner courtyard of a block close to downtown Zurich. It is a space he uses to create sketches and models and contemplate his projects in solitude; his staff works in an office located elsewhere. A neat, clean room, all it contains is sketches, drawings, models, and art books. On the wall hangs a sculpture by Hans Josephsohn (seen in the background of the photo on p. 102). This is the first time I have visited an atelier that was so "atelier"-like: a private ambience with just the right degree of tension. To create his projects, Märkli feels it is important to separate his thinking space (i.e., atelier) from the space where he talks with collaborators and draws up plans (i.e., office).

　Märkli spoke a lot about history. He declared that while it is not possible to further develop the architecture of Mies, that can be done with the architecture of the Renaissance and Palladio; also, the only difference between contemporary and Renaissance buildings is that ours are more comfortable. Instead of a Modernism that seeks to rewrite the present and express its future, he espouses the possibility of applying today a Renaissance outlook that renews the glories of the past. He asserts that this can be achieved by studying the past on one's own to determine why historical structures turned out the way they did, without concerning oneself with the intentions or theories of architects. A look at Märkli's work makes it clear that this is not just a form of conservatism. The point is to cultivate the abundant resources of both past and present without getting caught up in the ideology of newness. While this is not so easy to grasp as one does a clearly articulated con-

る社会や環境に強い関心が寄せられている。「building culture = 建物文化」。われわれはつい有名建築や建築家を参照して建築文化（architectural culture）や建築家の文化（architect's culture）ばかりを話してしまうが、そうではない。文化とはありとあらゆるすべての人がかかわるものなのである。建物はクライアントやユーザーだけのものではないし、もちろん建築家だけに向けたものでもない。さらには現代人だけでなく未来の人々にとっての遺産にもなりえる。建物を考えること、つくること、経験することはどれも文化にかかわることであり、あらゆる人が「建物文化」にかかわっている。今日の巨大資本は文化になんの貢献もしていないとメルクリが指摘するのはその通りだと思うが、現代において「建物文化」はいかに可能か、自分も考えてみたいと思った。

cept like modernism, these words of Märkli left a strong impression on me: "I stick to an understanding of human beings as they have existed until now."

Another point he made, citing La Congiunta as an example in our conversation, is that his work is concerned not with buildings alone, but with the society and environment in which they function. We tend to speak of "architectural culture" or "architect's culture" in reference to famous buildings and architects, but the "building culture" Märkli talks about is not like that. Culture, he maintains, is something that involves everyone. A building does not belong just to the client or the user, nor does it exist at the architect's pleasure. Nor is it only for our contemporaries: it may also be a legacy for our descendants. When we consider buildings, we must realize that both their construction and the experience of using them are a part of culture, and that all kinds of people participate in this "building culture." I agree with Märkli's assertion that today's big money makes no contribution to culture, but it leaves me wondering how we can make "building culture" a reality in the present era.

Novartis Campus Visitor Center / Basel, Switzerland / 2006

Peter Märkli

Peter Märkli

ノバルティス・キャンパス・ビジターセンター
Novartis Campus Visitor Center

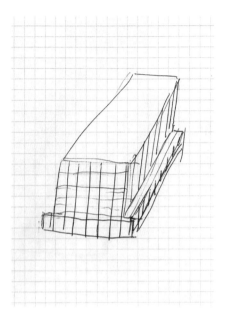
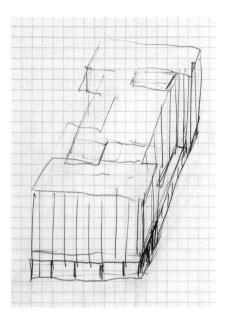
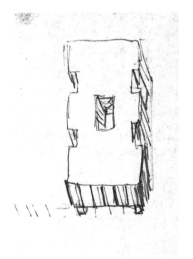

Peter Märkli

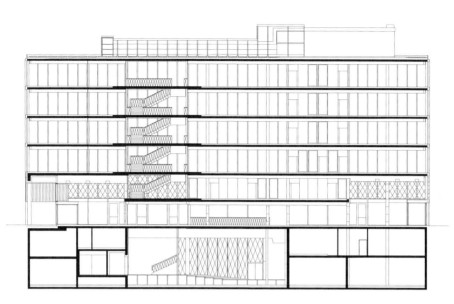

断面図　1:500
section 1:500

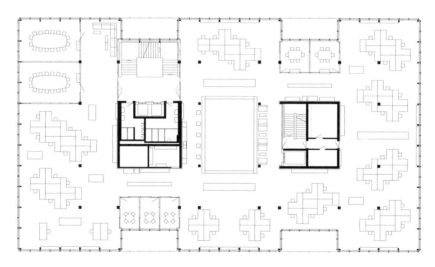

4階平面図　1:500
fourth floor plan 1:500

Peter Märkli

ノバルティス・キャンパス・ビジターセンター
Novartis Campus Visitor Center

Peter Märkli

Peter Märkli

138　シンセスの新施設／ゾロトゥルン、スイス／2012
Neubau Synthes／Solothurn, Switzerland／2012

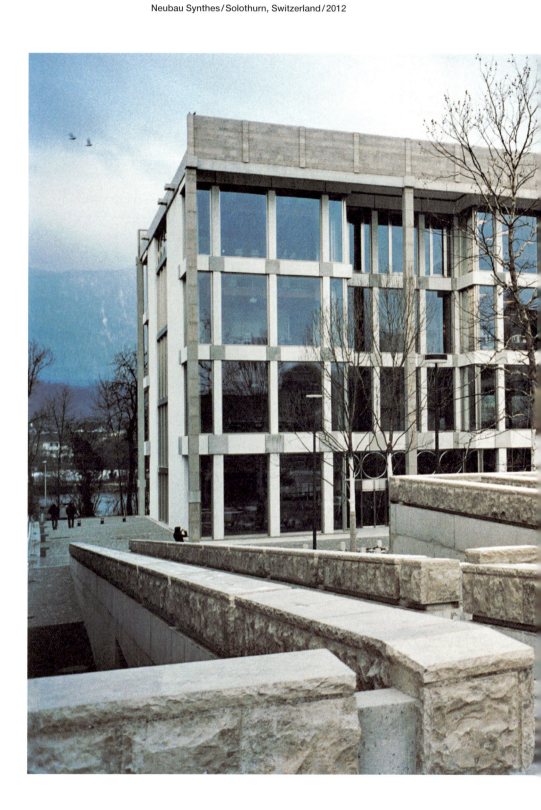

Peter Märkli

Peter Märkli

シンセスの新施設
Neubau Synthes

Peter Märkli

Anne Lacaton &
Jean-Philippe Vassal

10th March 2014
@ Lacaton & Vassal Architects, Paris, France

Anne Lacaton & Jean-Philippe Vassal

"Cheaper is more"

Go Hasegawa   Two weeks ago I saw a lecture by Mr. Vassal in Yokohama (International Symposium "Devising the City: Creative Neighborhoods vol. 2" on 23rd February 2014). You mentioned economy and I realized that Lacaton & Vassal have dealt with economy as a kind of method of being close to people and society. How did you arrive at that?

Jean-Philippe Vassal   By considering that economy is material. Today it's probably more interesting to work on economy than 50 years ago when it was done with normal materials—wood, concrete, or steel—whereas today these materials are no longer so important. It's much more a question of budgets. Because—I don't know if fortunately or unfortunately—society has mainly determined it as a goal, so we work within it. And we were really inspired by the evolution of architecture at one time with Mies van der Rohe's idea of "less is more," which today we could say also means "economical or cheaper is more."

We were very inspired by the Case Study Houses[1] in the U.S. in the fifties. That was real social housing dealing with contemporary and modern architecture, and how to live in it. It was nearly nothing, very small houses of steel, with a glass façade, one roof, that's all. But the quality of living there was very high. So with nearly nothing you can achieve the maximum. Today there are still these questions of minimum energy, minimum material, of standard materials but also minimum cost.

Anne Lacaton   We have been in a period of economic crisis for a few years—with difficulties finding the money to make things. We can see that in many cases or places this leads to making less, to reducing everything. Not only the very big projects commissioned by governments or cities—often the reduction is of more domestic, basic programs such as housing or facilities that everybody needs for daily life, like schools or hospitals. It's also very difficult as an architect to accept this situation, to accept that we should make very small housing, or fewer schools, or lots of things like that for people, just because we are in a time of crisis. This situation means that we have to figure out how to build in different ways, how to think about the space of a single project, how to use various techniques, how to do the maximum within a budget. It's very interesting and it brings about new approaches and a lot of invention.

GH I see. "Cheaper is more" is a very clear statement. But sometimes an architect has an opportunity where he has to make a building that doesn't look cheap in order to show off the fortune of the client, for instance, right? If a multimillionaire like Roman Abramovich asks you to make that sort of expensive building, how do you deal with it?

AL Since we've never been asked, we cannot know that! But expensive is not a contradiction of cheap. What is important is not the amount you have to spend, but how it's used and what you give for this amount. Spending a lot of money is not in itself a problem. It does not mean to make something bad. The only question is the intention, what it is done for—and if it's honest, if it's correct, if it's respectful of everything, if there is an ethic, if it makes sense. Of course we would judge that. And also if the client has intentions that we feel we can work with, if he seems nice to work with, if he is respectful, sympathetic—these are all criteria we would try to take into account if such a case came up.

JPV We think of economy not only for economy, but also because economy allows ambition. We see that more and more today, ambitions are restricted; programs are very often done at a minimum and cannot satisfy future needs. But due to the reduction of the money available to make projects, these restrictions appear as the only solutions. So we think that there is no reason today for architects to work on projects with this sort of minimum—minimum comfort, minimum surface, minimum light—that defines more and more architecture. The direct relationship between cost and project must be reconsidered and overstepped. This requires new approaches.

At this point, architecture and urbanism should be closer to seeing the opportunities and capacities of cities to provide possibilities for ambitious and generous projects. It is also a way to think about the opportunities of the city. Perhaps instead of making a new street or new electricity network, it is better to develop a new capacity for an existing street or improve the existing energy network.

This general economy of the city is very interesting, and by working in very precise architectural situations we can start to find solutions for some specific problems of the city through architecture, which then leads to urbanism. It means that we have to make better use of resources and existing capacities.

AL   Economy in a project doesn't mean just making it cheaper, but rather, making more for the same cost. This involves many parameters. But this is not the starting point. This is not the goal of the project. The economy of the project is a necessary tool to allow and accomplish intentions and the generosity that a project must provide. This is important, because a project in itself is not the result only of the intention of economy. The Latapie House (1993) [fig.1], the School of Architecture in Nantes [fig.2-4] (2009), and the Bois-le-Prêtre Tower Block Transformation (2011) are the result of intentions about quality of living, generosity of space, freedom of use.

If the intention had been just to reduce the cost, we would not have provided this double extra space, and these large open spaces, which we think are so important and so necessary for use and for appropriation. The work on the economy has made it possible to fulfill intentions and achieve them without diminishing or compromising them.

Largeness and pragmatism

GH   In practice you often propose doubling the size of a request within the same budget. What do you actually expect from the largeness of a space?

JPV   One gets more freedom, more possibilities in a larger space than in a smaller one. For the inhabitants it's freer, easier for living. And besides, it makes it easier to work on acoustic or thermic questions if you have these bigger spaces. Also, at the moment, we think it's interesting because we like the idea of not being constrained by rules—rules that often lead to the minimum—but to have more possibilities by introducing a kind of nomadic experience of space. To have this nomadic experience is clearly easier in a large space than in a small one. This idea is also related to the question of density. As architects or urbanists, we think that density doesn't mean more constraints of space, but that density should offer more possibilities to each family, to each person, to have more space for themselves. I really like this idea that the optimization of urban space (that is, density) works in balance with an increase of individual space.

AL   A large space allows us to decompress programs that are very often too small. The objective is to develop extra activities that would not be possible within the frame of the normal program, to provide possibilities of appropriation and imagination.

The School of Architecture in Nantes is an example. The plan for a studio for

25 students was 60 square meters. If you imagine what a school of architecture is, a place for learning and experimenting, this studio of 60 square meters wouldn't really allow experimentation.

Thus, for us it was important to say that a minimum of 60 extra square meters would be necessary in order to properly support teaching and experimentation, and we worked hard on the project to make this extra space possible without any extra cost.

We had the same intentions for the Social Housing in Mulhouse (2005); our goal was to change the standards of minimum living space and to build dwellings twice as big. If you look at the photos of the dwellings now, you can see how people use this large space very easily. They feel free in the space. The extra space allows them, for example, to have lunch in three or four places, according to the weather or one's desire. This freedom definitely provides a better quality of life. That's a very nice situation. It's a kind of luxury that we can offer in the context of social housing.

JPV   Today, unfortunately, a building is defined by its function. And this function is made from a lot of little functions inside, which makes a program, which is always at a minimum. In general, the building is nothing but the program. So you only have rooms with specific functions and no space around them, no air, no space that allows you to transcend the program, to change it.

In the end, a program is a compromise between real needs and an average cost determined, in general, by habit, without any precision. This lack of precision always leads to restricting the program. And this becomes an unquestionable reality. Large spaces are also interesting for the community and for the social relationships in the community. It's very important to have something to share.

GH   That's interesting. A large space is also your way of contributing to many things—the user's freedom, quality of life, possibilities, community.

Then, I want to ask you this question: Do you think architecture can change society?

AL   Is it the role of architecture to change society? That might be too much power. What we think is more important, as architects, is to try to understand the changes of the society, its needs, expectations, and desires, and to provide spaces—private or public—that are not restrictive or constraining on a way of life, but allow inhabitants the freedom to make the life they desire.

JPV   What we are pretty sure of, anyway, is that the Latapie House had an influence on the Latapie family. And we know, for example, that the students at the Nantes School now have formed more than 15 associations—five times more than before, and with a lot of proposals for activities and events. So this means that space can probably open up initiatives, some possibilities.

GH   I see. From what you say it seems to me your attitude toward architecture is always very clear, and pragmatic in the positive sense.

JPV   Yes. For example, what do you think of the D House in Lége-Cap-Ferret (1998)? [fig.5, 6]

GH   In the case of that project's story, my impression was not one of pragmatism, I guess.

JPV   The story of this project is that you can dream. It's like a dream that you can preserve all the trees and just make the house without cutting the trees. It's nearly utopian.

Once you decide to be utopian but you realize you need to be pragmatic, being pragmatic doesn't mean that you cannot be extremely ambitious. For me that is very important. You can have a poetic approach to space, to life, to architecture, and at the same time be pragmatic, precise, thrifty. It is not contradictory. If anything, it is complementary.

We think that there is a combination of energy, time, permanence, and pragmatism that we must maintain in order to have nice ambitious results in the end. In the countryside, where people are working in the fields, they have to be very patient to ensure that they have good products ten months later. It is exciting to be very ambitious. We are interested in the architecture and urbanism of the sixties because we have the feeling that often those architects were very generous in their objectives. They have to be considered a sort of utopia. Perhaps at that time it was technically difficult. But I think today we should look at these ideas again with a fresh gaze, a lot of precision and interest, and, precisely, with pragmatism.

AL   Often in the context of architecture, pragmatism is not considered a positive notion—it would mean that what is pragmatic is not very creative.

But in a way, the architects who worked on utopian ideas in the fifties or sixties never built those utopias because they lacked the rigor and pragmatism to achieve them. It's a pity that all these projects have not been built. We would really like to see Cedric Price's[2] the Fun Palace (1961) [fig.7] or other projects like that one today. We know that it is really necessary to have dreams, to have generosity, to have ambitious intentions, and then to have creativity and inventiveness. But it's also necessary to have the seriousness and pragmatism to bring all those ideas to completion.

JPV   I like the idea of art. As an architect you are close to art, which is not the way an engineer would work. You make things with emotion, sensibility, a poetic approach, but also a precise approach with a lot of rigor, precision, and pragmatism. It is very important to have this in mind, and you try to develop your personal art. That's why what we are doing is different from what other architects are doing. We believe in our way of doing this work of architecture because we know that other people will live there and appropriate the space, and we are really interested in that.

Very often we read that we don't care about aesthetics... We care about aesthetics! We are just confident that, from the way we design and build our projects, step by step, with a lot of care in the use of space and relationships from inside to outside, we will have a very precise and interesting aesthetic at the end. It's not an aesthetic that is defined at the first step of the design, but one that appears when everything is finished. We are confident in this approach. But aesthetic sensibility is important, because it hopefully makes the city more beautiful.

People's life, and the lightness of architecture

GH The photographs of your works are very different from those of other architects. They show the ordinary life of people and also a freedom from control by the architect. You did this from the beginning with the Latapie House, and I was very surprised to see it when I was a student. There were very ordinary plastic chairs, objects belonging to clients... a very light and pleasant ambience.

JPV I think projects are mainly for people to live in, for inhabitants, wherever they are. They are not masterpieces only seen in architectural magazines [fig.8].

People must be free inside their space. They must feel comfortable, appropriate the space for themselves, and like the space. They have to develop their skills and their ability to decorate, to place flowers, to buy furniture, to use the space following their desire. The spaces that we propose need to have some qualities that we try to provide. Qualities of light, comfort, qualities that will give pleasure to the inhabitants—and also, a place that will be important and friendly to them. A place you can change and move, not a place you cannot touch or you have to be very careful with. It's something that you can use, that you can live in... A space has to be friendly and welcoming to its inhabitants, because most of the time it's their space. It's no longer the space of the architect.

GH That's why in your lecture in Yokohama you said at the beginning, "We think from the inside."

JPV Yes, we think like that and we design like that. It's important from the outside too, but if we imagine the construction of a space or deal with the necessities, the needs and wishes of each inhabitant—it's always from the inside.

Even when we are outside of the building, we are inside the street, so in fact we are always inside. We cannot consider the building as an outside object. That doesn't interest us. How it looks outside is just a result of how it is done from the inside. And probably the outside of the building will change a lot if the inhabitants open or close their winter gardens, or if they place some flowers on the balcony or if the curtain is red instead of blue.

It's an image that results from the project and from what the inhabitants do in the space and how they use the space. What we see is surprising sometimes, but we are interested in those kinds of surprises.

GH   Your buildings always look very light, and this is very different from other European architects, especially other French architects, I think.

AL   Yes, it is true.

GH   Yes, sometimes I sense more of an affinity in your work with Japanese architecture than with French architects.

JPV   For a long time we have been fascinated by the houses of Kazuo Shinohara[3]. There is a kind of obviousness in the landscape—the simplicity, the perfection and the strength of the interior space.

The sliding door, an element of Japanese architecture, is very interesting for us—these partitions that appear and disappear. It's from traditional Japanese architecture, but it's still used in modern architecture in Japan. I think it's interesting the way one space opens to another space, or a space opens to outside space.

We like to work with light and with the sun. So we design projects that catch the light and the sun as much as we can in the space. The result is what you might call an "architecture of light." It brings transparency and openness. After that, we have curtains and winter gardens which allow us to filter the light gradually. We work with intermediate buffer zones.

But always we maintain the possibility of this maximum transparency towards the outside. And it is also our method to work on energy savings with passive systems, bioclimates, intermediate spaces, instead of what is generally advocated and done in France today: small windows in concrete façades with a thick exterior foam insulation.

AL   To cut contact with the outside to the minimum possible. That's what the regulations lead one to make in Europe nowadays.

JPV   But in a way, that brings us back to your question. From the outside we wish to let the life of people living inside appear, with some plants or furniture or curtains. I think that's also important in the buildings by Kazuyo Sejima[4], for example.

What we try to do is always to provide this possibility of escape so that your eyes can go as far as possible. To extend the space so that it provides time to move inside, from one point to another. That feeling is also related to the question of lightness, giving the feeling that you can breathe, that you are free. That's related to pleasure, to well-being. We think it's important for people not to always be in a space where they feel too much materiality.

GH Do you actually feel an affinity with contemporary Japanese architects?

AL What is interesting in some contemporary architecture in Japan, such as that of SANAA or Toyo Ito[5], is this feeling of lightness, of suspension.

It seems more relaxed with the rules than we are. It seems more possible for these architects to make an intelligent structure with a lot of care about the use, the quality of life inside, the landscape. It's well built, but it doesn't seem so determined, so constrained by the rules as it is here, by lots of standards. And that's very interesting and enviable.

Superposition of times and contexts

GH You mentioned the influence of the Case Study Houses in the U.S. in the fifties. As architects, what do you think about architectural history?

JPV We travel quite a lot. And we are curious, we like to look, to listen. Observation is very interesting and that is why it is so interesting to visit other countries. We try to understand what we see. The curiosity is not only about architecture, but also about space, landscapes. That is important and we try to keep this experience as a part of the context of our ideas. We are also interested in modern architecture. We really think that Modernism is something important, because it is part of our time. But it's always in addition, it's always complementary to the old architecture, old urbanism, old situations... We are interested in all these contexts and the superposition of all times and contexts.

AL We don't see history as the past, but much more as a permanent continuity which recreates permanently a new contemporary situation.

JPV We like not only modern architecture but also many other things, such as some historical urban systems. For example the development of very old Italian villages: how they have grown, layer upon layer, how they have become whole cities like Perugia. We are interested in questions of climate, for example how a straw hut is adapted to a particular part of Africa. Or in Granada, how it is possible for the gardens to be so fresh just with water when the air outside is so hot. These elements are also tools with which to understand and work with the things we were talking about: economy, ecology, sustainability, pleasure or comfort, and art.

What is important, I think, is to learn from what we see. For example, Next 21 in Osaka (1993) is in the end not interesting as a finished building, but the research and the experience were really important and fundamental for us. So we try to look at which paths can be interesting and always look at things with this optimistic point of view.

GH   You see history as a sort of architectural material that you can actively study, like economy as you mentioned at the beginning. And you don't see history from above like a god, you always try to participate in it. History with a practical view. That is your sense of history.

JPV   Yes, I think precision is a necessity, and very often when you look down from above you do not have enough precision. It's really good to try to understand situations very precisely, why something was successful or unsuccessful, to understand all the elements and their relations, and then to take your material and your tools from that.

1 —— Case Study Houses: A series of experimental houses organized by an architecture magazine publisher in America to address the surge in housing demand after the Second World War. Charles and Ray Eames, Craig Ellwood, Pierre Koenig, Eero Saarinen, Richard Neutra, and other famous architects participated and realized many projects.
2 —— Cedric Price: British architect born in 1934 and deceased in 2003. Also an educator at AA School, he proposed new architecture through unbuilt works that addressed information science and technology. He is best known for "Fun Palace" and "Potteries Thinkbelt," produced in the 1960s.
3 —— Kazuo Shinohara: Japanese architect born in 1925 and deceased in 2006. Major works include Umbrella House (1961) and Tokyo Institute of Technology Centennial Hall (1987). He is also known for authoring *Houses and Architectural Theory* (1970).
4 —— Kazuyo Sejima: Japanese architect born in 1956. In the 1980's, she worked for Toyo Ito. She established SANAA with Ryue Nishizawa (born 1966). Major works include Saishunkan Seiyaku Women's Dormitory (1991) and House in a Plum Grove (2003).
5 —— Toyo Ito: Japanese architect born in 1941. After having worked for Kiyonori Kikutake in the late 1960's, he established his own practice. Best known for White U (House in Nakano-Shinmachi) (1976), Sendai Mediatheque (2000), and Taichung Opera House (2015) to name a few.

アンヌ・ラカトン ＆
ジャン=フィリップ・ヴァッサル

2014年3月10日
フランス、パリ、ラカトン＆ヴァッサル・アーキテクツにて

「より安いことは、より豊かなこと（Cheaper is more）」

長谷川豪（以下、GH）　私は2週間前に横浜でジャン・フィリップ・ヴァッサルさんのレクチャー（国際シンポジウム「都市を仕掛ける――住環境が新しい社会をつくる」vol.2、2014年2月23日）に伺いました。レクチャーでは経済性に関する話題がありましたね。お話を聞いていて、ラカトン＆ヴァッサルは、建築の経済性を人々や社会に近づくための手段として扱ってきたのだということに気がつきました。どのようにして、そのような考えに至ったのでしょうか。

ジャン=フィリップ・ヴァッサル（以下、JPV）　私たちは経済性を材料だと考えています。経済性について取り組むことは、おそらく50年前よりもずっと面白いはずです。以前までは、木材やコンクリート、鉄骨といった普通の材料が建築に用いられてきました。しかし今日では、これらの材料はもうそれほど重要ではありません。むしろ、いま課題とされているのは材料ではなく、予算です。喜ぶべきか悲しむべきかわかりませんが、現代社会ではほとんどの場合、経済的な最終目標がすでに決まっていて、私たちはその枠組みのなかで働いています。かつて、ミース・ファン・デル・ローエが「より少ないことは、より豊かなこと（Less is more）」と発言した時代には、私たちは建築の進化に大いに触発されてきました。しかし今日では、「Less is more」は「より経済的、より安いことは、より豊かなことだ（Economical or cheaper is more）」とも言い換えられるでしょう。
　私たちは1950年代のアメリカのケース・スタディ・ハウス[1]に大きな影響を受けました。それは現代建築および近代建築をテーマにしながら、どのように住まう

かを考えた本当に社会的な住宅でした。最小限の操作のみの非常に小さな住宅で、鉄骨造でガラスファサードと屋根を備えたシンプルなものでした。しかし、この住宅で想定された生活の質はとても高かったのです。ほぼ最小限といえる操作が、最大限の効果をもたらしたのです。今日課題とされ、取り組まれているのは、標準的な材料を用いて、エネルギーや材料の量を最小限に抑えることだけでなく、コストを最小限に抑えることも課題となっています。

アンヌ・ラカトン（以下、AL） この数年のあいだ経済的な危機の時期にあり、ものをつくるための資金を得ることも困難でした。そのため、つくるものの量を減らし、すべてを縮小する方針に繋がることが多くなりました。政府あるいは地方自治体が委託する大規模プロジェクトだけでなく、市民の日常生活に必要な施設、例えば住宅、学校や病院といった身近で基本的なプログラムも、縮小されることが多いのです。建築家にとっては、このような状況を受け入れるのは難しいことです。経済危機だからという理由で、人々のために狭小住宅や限られた数の学校ばかりを建てるべきではありません。このような状況下では、さまざまな方法で建てること、ひとつのプロジェクトにおける空間のあり方、多様な技術の使い方、予算を最大限に活かす方法などについて考える必要があります。こうした過程はとても刺激的で、新しいアプローチやアイデアを私たちにもたらしてくれます。

GH そうですね。「より安いことは、より豊かなこと」という表現は非常に明快にお二人のスタンスを示しています。しかし建築家は、ときにはクライアントの資産を誇示するために、安っぽく見えない建物をつくらなければならない時もありませんか？ 例えばもしロマン・アブラモヴィッチのような億万長者にそのような高価な建物を依頼されたら、どのように対応しますか？

AL そのような高価な建物の設計依頼を受けたことがないので、想像がつきませんね！ でも、「高い」ということは、「安い」ということの対義ではないのです。重要なのは使うお金の額ではなく、そのお金をどのように使い、なにを提供するかということです。不正に使うような場合は別ですが、多額のお金を使うこと自体にはなんの問題もありません。唯一問うべきはその目的、つまりなんのために使うのかということです。誠実で正しい目的のために、すべてに敬意を払っており、倫理に基づいていて意味のあるものかどうか、が問われるのです。私たちは、当然こうした基準に従って判断します。また、クライアントの目的が私たちの仕事上の興味をかきたてるものであると同時に、そのクライアントと一緒に仕事をしたいと思える

fig.1 ラタピ邸(1993)
Latapie House, 1993

ような、敬意を払うことのできる人物であることが大事です。高価な建物の案件に出会った場合には、こういった条件を基準にして判断するでしょう。

JPV　私たちが経済性について考えるのは、経済性自体に興味があるからというだけでなく、経済性によってさまざまな欲望が達成されるからです。今日、欲望はますます抑制されています。例えば、建物のプログラムは最小限に抑えられることが多いのですが、これでは、将来に生じる必要性を満たせない可能性があります。プロジェクトにあてられる資金が減少しているため、このように制限するしか方法がないのでしょうが。私たちは、現代の建築家たちがこのような「最小限」の考えでプロジェクトに取り組むのは合理的ではないと思っています。最小限の快適性、最小限の外観、最小限の採光といった要素が建築に多くみられるようになっています。しかし、コストとプロジェクトの直接的な関係を再考し、限界を乗り越えなくてはなりません。そのためには新たなアプローチが必要です。

　いまは、建築とアーバニズムのあいだにより密接な関係をつくりだし、都市の持っている能力や都市にあるさまざまな機会を探り、意欲的で大きなプロジェクトの可能性を提供すべきです。それは都市にどのようなチャンスがあるかを考えることでもあります。おそらく、新しい街路や電力ネットワークをつくるよりも、既存の街路やエネルギー・ネットワークの新しい可能性を見出すほうが有益でしょう。

　都市全体の経済性という考え方は注目に値するものです。都市における問題解決を具体的な建築を通じて探求した結果が、都市のほかの部分に適用できることもあ

りますし、そのことがアーバニズムに繋がっていくでしょう。ですから、私たちはもっと、リソースやすでに存在する能力をうまく使っていく必要があります。

AL　プロジェクトにおける節約とは、単により安くすることではなく、むしろ同じコストをより有効に活用するということです。これにはたくさんのパラメーターが含まれています。経済性はスタート地点ではありませんし、ゴールでもありません。プロジェクトにおける経済性とは、プロジェクトの目的やプロジェクトが持つべきおおらかさを達成するために必要なツールなのです。プロジェクトは経済的な目的さえ達成すればよいわけではありませんから、経済性はツールとして重要なのです。《ラタピ邸》（1993）[fig.1]、《ナント建築学校》（2009）[fig.2-4]、《ボワ・ル・プレートル高層住宅の改修》（2011）は、良質な生活、空間のおおらかさ、自由な使い方を意図した成果です。

　もしコスト削減だけを目的としていれば、これらの事例でみられるような、2倍の空間を設けたり、大きなオープンスペースを設けたりといったことはしなかったでしょう。大きなオープンスペースは、自由な使い方や空間配分のためにとても重要だと私たちは考えています。私たちが意図したことを減らしたり妥協することなく、プロジェクトを完成させるためには経済性について考えることが必要不可欠なのです。

大きさとプラグマティズム

GH　お二人は実際に同じ予算内で、所要面積の2倍の面積を提案することが多いですね。これらは空間の大きさになにを期待してのことなのでしょうか。

JPV　空間を大きくすると、より多くの自由が得られます。大きな空間には、小さな空間よりも多くの可能性があるのです。また、居住者は、より自由で気楽に暮らせるようになります。そのほかにも、大きな空間のほうが音響あるいは断熱といった問題に取り組みやすいといった利点もあるでしょう。たいてい規則のせいで最小限のことしかできないのですが、いまのところその規則に縛られないという自分たちの姿勢や、遊牧民のような空間体験を提案することでより大きな可能性を示すことができる点が気に入っています。小さな空間よりも大きな空間のほうが、遊牧民のような体験をしやすいということは明白で、この考えは密度の問題にも関係しています。私たちは建築家あるいはアーバニストとして、密度によって空間を制限するばかりでなく、それぞれの家族や居住者が、より多くの空間を自分たちのために

fig.2, 3　ナント建築学校（2009）
School of Architecture in Nantes, 2009

Anne Lacaton & Jean-Philippe Vassal

持つという可能性を高めるべきで、個人の空間を増やしていくバランスのなかで、都市空間、都市の密度が最適化するという考え方がとても気に入っているのです。

AL　大きな空間によって、足りていないプログラムを適切な規模に戻すこともできます。ときには通常のプログラムの枠組みでは不可能な、特別なアクティヴィティを展開させ、新しい空間配分の方法や想像力の可能性を生み出すこともあります。

　その事例のひとつが《ナント建築学校》です。25名の学生のためのスタジオは、当初の想定では60m^2でした。しかし、学習と実験的な活動の場である建築学校ということを考慮すれば、この60m^2のスタジオだと、実験的な活動はまったくできないことがわかるでしょう。

　そこで、教育や実験的な活動を適切に行なうためには、最低でもさらに60m^2の空間を追加する必要があると主張しました。それと同時に、追加された空間を、追加の工事費なしで実現できるように取り組みました。

　《ミュールーズの公営住宅》(2005)においても同じように考えました。私たちの目的は最小限の居住空間の基準を変えること、そして住戸を2倍の大きさで建てることでした。人々が居住している写真を見ると、この大きな空間を住人がいかにうまく使いこなしているかがわかるでしょう。彼らはこの空間に自由を感じているのです。この追加された空間を活かし、天候や気分によって、昼食をあちこちでとることができます。こうした自由により、生活の質が確実に向上するのです。それはとてもよい状況ですし、公営住宅においても、このような贅沢を提供できるのです。

JPV　今日では残念ながら、建物は機能によって定義されます。機能はさらに小さな機能の集合でできています。小さな機能とはプログラムのことですが、プログラムはつねに最小限しかありません。一般的に建物とはプログラムにすぎないのです。だから、特定の機能を持った部屋があるのみで、その周りを囲む空間——プログラムを変えたり、プログラムを超えた使い方ができるような空間——などないのです。

　結局、プログラムとは現実的な需要と平均的な費用のあいだの妥協であり、一般的には正当性ではなく慣習で決められるものです。正当性が欠如した状態では、たいていはプログラムが制限される傾向にあります。そしてそのまま現実のものになっていくのです。ですから、大きな空間は、コミュニティやその内部での社会的な関係性という側面からみても興味深いものなのです。シェアできるものを持つと

fig.4 ナント建築学校
School of Architecture in Nantes

Anne Lacaton & Jean-Philippe Vassal

Anne Lacaton & Jean-Philippe Vassal

いうことは、とても大事ですから。

GH とても興味深いですね。大きな空間によって利用者の自由、生活の質、さまざまな可能性、コミュニティなど、じつにさまざまなことに応えようとしているのですね。
　では、あなたたちは建築によって社会を刷新することができると思いますか？

AL 社会を刷新するということは、建築の役割なのでしょうか？　社会を刷新する力というのは、大げさすぎるかもしれません。
　建築家としてもっと大事なことは、社会の変化、ニーズ、期待そして欲望を理解すること、そして利用者がライフスタイルを変えることなく、彼らが望む生活を——プライヴェートあるいはパブリックどちらの空間としても——自由に過ごせる場所を提供することだと、私たちは考えます。

JPV いずれにせよ、《ラタピ邸》はラタピ家に影響を与えたと私たちは確信しています。そして《ナント建築学校》はいまでは15以上の組織（以前の5倍）が結成され、たくさんのアクティヴィティやイヴェントの提案もあります。つまり、空間が自発性や新しい可能性を誘発しているということです。

GH なるほど。ここまでお話を聞いていて、あなたたちの建築に対する態度はつねにとても明快で、そしてポジティヴな意味でプラグマティックですね。

JPV そうですね、でも例えば《キャップ・フェレのD邸》(1998) [fig.5, 6] に対してあなたはどのような印象を持ちましたか？

GH あのプロジェクトに関してはプラグマティックな印象はないかもしれないですね。

JPV プロジェクトのストーリーは夢想的なものです。林のなかですべての木を保存し、かつ木を切ることもなしに家をつくることができるという、ユートピアン的な夢です。
　ユートピアンになると決意したあとに、同時にプラグマティックである必要に気づいたとしても、プラグマティックであることと極限まで野心的であるということは両立できるのです。私にとって、これはとても大事なことです。空間や生活、そ

fig.5 キャップ・フェレのD邸 (1998)
D House in Lége-Cap-Ferret, 1998

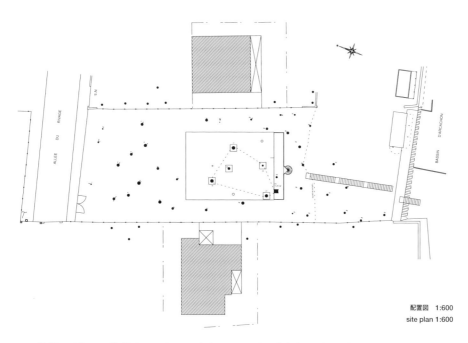

配置図 1:600
site plan 1:600

して建築に対して詩的なアプローチをしつつも、同時にプラグマティックであり、正確であり、そして倹約することは可能なのです。矛盾するのではなく、むしろ互いを補い合うことができます。

　最終的に素晴らしい野心的な結果を得るためには、エネルギー、時間、不変性、プラグマティズムといったものを組み合わせて、持ち続けることが大事だと考えています。田舎の人々は、10カ月後によい作物を収穫するために、畑で忍耐強く働くのです。野心的であるということはエキサイティングです。私たちは1960年代の建築やアーバニズムに興味があります。この時期の建築家たちは、非常に大きな目標を持っていたと感じるからです。それはある種のユートピア思想と考えるべきですが、当時はおそらく技術的に難しかったことでも、いまではプラグマティズムを伴った新たな視点、精度や関心などからこうしたアイデアを見ることができると思います。

AL　建築のコンテクストにおいては、プラグマティズムは前向きな概念ではないと考えられることが多いのです。別の言い方をすれば、プラグマティックであるということはクリエイティヴではないと捉えられているのです。

　しかし考えようによっては、1950年代や60年代のユートピア的なアイデアに取り組んでいた建築家たちが、ユートピアを建設することがなかったのは、彼らにはユートピアの実現に必要だった厳格さや実践力が備わっていなかったからだとも言

Anne Lacaton & Jean-Philippe Vassal

fig.6 キャップ・フェレのD邸
D House in Lége-Cap-Ferret

Anne Lacaton & Jean-Philippe Vassal

fig.7 セドリック・プライス「ファン・パレス」(1961)
Cedric Price, Fun Palace, 1961

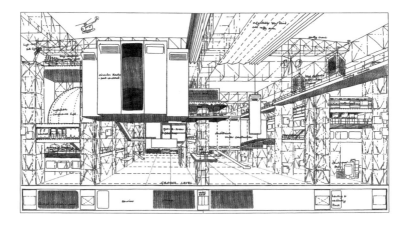

えます。これらのプロジェクトが建てられなかったのは残念です。セドリック・プライス[2]の「ファン・パレス」(1961) [fig.7]、あるいはそれに類する別のプロジェクトをぜひいつか見てみたいものです。私たちは、夢、おおらかさ、野心的な目的、そして創造性と進歩性を持つことがきわめて重要だと考えています。そして、プラグマティックにこれらのアイデアを完成に導かなければいけないと思います。

JPV 私はアートの考え方が好きです。建築家はエンジニアの考え方とは違い、アーティストにより近いのです。物事を感情、感受性、詩的なアプローチを持って考えると同時に、厳格さと正確さ、そしてプラグマティズムを備えたアプローチをします。この事実を心に留めておくことはとても大事ですし、そこから自分のアートを発展させようと試みています。だから、私たちがやっていることはほかの建築家たちがやっていることと違うと言われるのでしょう。私たちは、自分たちの建築の仕事のやり方を信じています。なぜなら、自分たち以外の人々が実際に住んで、その空間を自分のものにしていくということを知っていますし、そのことにとても興味があるからです。

　また、私たちには美学についての配慮がないと書かれているのを、よく目にします……。けれども私たちは美学を大事にしているのです！　私たちがプロジェクトをデザインして建てていくプロセスにおいて、空間の使い方や、内部と外部の関係性におおいに配慮して一歩一歩進めていけば、最後には適切で興味深い美学を体現できると確信しているのです。美学とはデザインの最初の段階で決まるものではな

fig.8 ボワ・ル・プレートル高層住宅の改修(2011)
Bois-le-Prêtre Tower Block Transformation, 2011

く、すべてが完成したときに現われるものです。私たちはこのアプローチに自信を持っています。美的な感受性は重要です。それによって都市がより美しくなることを期待できるからです。

人々の生活と建築の軽やかさ

GH　いまの美学についてのお話に関連すると思いますが、あなたたちの作品の写真はほかの建築家のものとだいぶ違います。人々の普通の生活、建築家のコントロールから解放された状態が撮影されています。初期の《ラタピ邸》からこのようなやり方でしたが、私は学生時代にその写真をみて、とても驚いたのです。ごく普通のプラスティックの椅子やクライアントの日用品が置いてあって、とても気軽で、幸せな雰囲気があります。

JPV　どのようなプロジェクトでも、基本的にはその場所に住む人、その場所にいる人々のためのものだと私は考えています。建築雑誌でしか見ることのできない名作建築ではなく、実際に住んでいる人がいるのです [fig.8]。
　人々は、住宅のなかでは自由でいるべきです。快適に過ごし、住宅を自分たちなりに住みこなし、空間に愛着をもつ。装飾したり、花を飾ったり、家具を買ったり、思いどおりに空間を使うためのスキルを磨かなくてはなりません。私たちが提案する空間は、良質な条件を備えているはずです。光、快適性、そして居住者に歓びを

もたらす良質さ。それから、居住者にとって、愛着が湧くような、親しみやすい場所であることも大事です。自分たちで変更を加えることができる場所であるべきで、触ってはいけなかったり、こまごまとした注意事項があるような場所ではいけません。使い、住むための空間なのです。空間は基本的に居住者のものですから、親しみやすくいつでも受け入れてくれるものでなくてはならないのです。そして完成した住宅は、もはや建築家のものではありません。

GH　だからあなたは横浜でのレクチャーで最初に、「私たちは内側から考えます（We think from the inside）」とおっしゃったのですね。

JPV　そうです。私たちはそのように考え、デザインします。外側から考えることも大事です。しかし、実際の空間の建設、あるいは必要条件、それぞれの居住者のニーズや希望への対応、こういったものはつねに内側から発生するものだと考えます。

　私たちが建物の外にいるときでも、街路の内側にいると言えますから、実際にはいつもなにかの内側にいると言えます。建物を外部にあるオブジェクトだと考えることはできません。私たちはそういった考え方には興味がないのです。外観が外側からどのように見えるかは、単に内側から成されたことの結果にすぎません。居住者がウィンター・ガーデンを開放したり、あるいはバルコニーに花を置いたりカーテンを青から赤に変えたりするだけで、建物の外観は変わるかもしれません。

　こういった外観の変化は、プロジェクトの結果として、そして居住者の行動や空間の使い方などからくるイメージです。このような変化を実際に目にして驚くこともありますが、それも面白いものです。

GH　あなたたちの建物はいつもとても軽やかに見えますが、これはヨーロッパのほかの建築家とはかなり違いますね。特にフランスの建築家としては異色だという印象があります。

AL　ええ、そうですね。

GH　あなたたちの作品が、フランスの建築家によるものというよりも日本の建築に近いと感じることもあります。

JPV　長いあいだ、私たちは篠原一男[3]の住宅に魅せられてきました。彼がつくる

風景のなかには、ある種の理解しやすい特徴があります。単純さ、完璧さ、そして内部空間の力です。

　引き戸は日本建築の要素ですが、私たちにとっても非常に興味深い要素です。戸が現われたり消えたりするのですから。伝統的な日本建築に由来していますが、日本の現代建築にも使われています。ひとつの空間が次の空間、あるいは外部に向かって開かれるという点で興味深いのです。

　私たちは光や太陽を扱うのが好きです。だから光や太陽をできるだけ空間に取り込むことのできるプロジェクトを設計します。結果的には「光の建築（architecture of light）」と呼べるようなものになり、透明性と開放性をもたらします。それから、光を段階的に透過するカーテンやウィンター・ガーデンを設けます。中間のバッファー・ゾーンについても検討します。

　通常は、外部への透明性を最大限に保ちます。フランスでは、分厚い外断熱用の発砲断熱材を施工したコンクリートのファサードに、小さな窓を設けるといった方法が一般的に行なわれています。ですが私たちはその代わりに、パッシヴ・システム、生気候（bioclimate）、バッファー・ゾーンといった方法で、エネルギー削減を検討しているのです。

AL　フランスの一般的な方法では、外部との接触を遮断し、なるべく最小限に留めます。現在の欧州では、法規に従うとこのようなかたちになります。

JPV　日本建築と私たちの建築の共通点の質問に戻りましょう。私たちは、植物や家具やカーテンなどを通して、内部の生活が外部に表われるといいなと願っています。そうした思いは例えば、妹島和世さん[4]の建築でも顕著に示されていると思います。

　また、私たちがつねに心がけているのは、引きのある場所をつくり、より遠くまで見渡せるようにすることです。空間を拡張することで、内部空間のある地点から別の地点へと動く時間を提供できます。その感覚はまたいきいきとして、自由にふるまうことのできる軽やかさ（lightness）ということにもかかわってきます。また、歓びや心身の健康にもかかわってきます。人々があまりにマテリアリティを感じる空間に、ずっと居座り続けないことが重要だと考えています。

GH　実際に、現代の日本の建築家たちに親近感を覚えますか？

AL　日本の現代建築の一部、例えばSANAAや伊東豊雄さん[5]などの建築で興味深

いのは、いまお話ししたような軽やかさや浮遊する感覚です。

　彼らは私たちよりも、規則に対してさらに柔軟に対応しているようです。こういった建築家たちは、使い方、内部の生活の質、ランドスケープなどに十分に配慮してつくることができるのでしょう。うまくつくられていて、決まりきった感じがなく、私たちの国の建築のような、さまざまな法規や基準による束縛を感じさせないように思います。とても面白いのはもちろんですし、羨ましくもあります。

すべての時代とコンテクストを重ね合わせること

GH　冒頭で1950年代のアメリカのケーススタディ・ハウスの影響について言及されました。建築家として、建築の歴史についてはどのようにお考えですか？

JPV　私たちはよく旅をします。好奇心旺盛で、いろいろなことを見聞するのが好きです。観察することに心惹かれ、外国を訪れるのはとても面白いものです。そうやって見たことを理解しようとしています。建築だけではなく、空間やランドスケープにも興味があります。こういった知見や経験はとても重要で、自分たちのアイデアの背景として蓄えておこうと思っています。モダニズム建築にも興味があります。モダニズムは現代の一部分でもあるので、重要だと考えているのです。しかしモダニズムはいつも、昔の建築やアーバニズム、昔の状況などに付随する、補完的な要素となっています。これらのすべてのコンテクスト、そしてすべての時代やコンテクストの重ね合わせにも興味があります。

AL　私たちは歴史を過去のものではなく、それ以上に、恒久的に今日的な状況をつくりだしていく永続的な連続性と捉えているのです。

JPV　私たちはモダニズム建築だけでなく、ほかのたくさんのもの、歴史的な都市のシステムなども好きです。例を挙げると、とても古いイタリアの村が、どのようにしてレイヤーの上にレイヤーを重ねながら発展し、ペルージャのようなひとつの都市になったのかといったことです。ほかにも、どのような経緯からわら葺き小屋がアフリカの特定の地域に適するようになっていったのかというような気候問題にも関心があります。あるいはスペイン南部のグラナダで外気温の高さにもかかわらず、どうやって水だけで庭園をいきいきとした状態に保てるのかといったことにも。こういったことは、すでにお話ししたような、経済、環境、サステイナビリティ、快楽や快適性、そしてアートについて理解するためのツールにもなります。

私たちは、実際に自分で見て学ぶことが大事だと考えています。大阪の《NEXT21》(1993) は、竣工した建物としては面白味に欠けるかもしれませんが、その過程でのリサーチや体験は私たちにとって非常に重要で、なくてはならないものでした。私たちはどのような方向に進めば面白いかを見定めようとしていますし、このような楽観的な見方でものごとを見ています。

GH 歴史を、冒頭で話されていた経済性と同様に、積極的に探求できる建築の材料として見なしているのですね。神のように歴史を上から見下ろすのではなく、つねにそのなかに参加しようとされています。プラクティカルな視点から見た歴史というのが、あなたの歴史に対するスタンスですね。

JPV はい。私は正確さが必要だと考えていますが、上から見下ろしただけでは充分に正確でないことが非常に多い。あることがなぜ成功したのか、あるいはなぜ成功しなかったのかといった状況を正確に理解しようとすること、そしてすべての要素や関係性を理解すること、そこから自分にとっての素材やツールを得ることはとてもよいことだと考えています。

1——ケース・スタディ・ハウス：第2次世界大戦後の住宅需要に応じるかたちで、アメリカの建築雑誌上で行なわれた実験住宅の企画。チャールズ＆レイ・イームズやクレイグ・コーニッグ、エーロ・サーリネン、リチャード・ノイトラら著名建築家が参加し、数々の実作が生みだされた。
2——セドリック・プライス(1934-2003)：イギリス出身の建築家。AAスクールの教師を務め、60年代には「ファン・パレス」(1961)や「ポタリーズ・シンクベルト計画」(1964)など、実現には至らなかったものの、情報科学技術を導入した新たな建築を提案した。
3——篠原一男(1925-2006)：日本の建築家。主な作品に《から傘の家》(1961)、《東京工業大学百年記念館》(1987)、著書に『住宅論』(SD選書、1970)などがある。
4——妹島和世(1956-)：日本の建築家。80年代に伊東豊雄に師事した。代表作に《再春館製薬女子寮》(1991)、《梅林の家》(2003)などがある。西沢立衛(1966-)とともにSANAAを主宰。
5——伊東豊雄(1941-)：日本の建築家。60年代後半に菊竹清訓に師事した後に独立した。代表作に《ホワイトU(中野本町の家)》(1976)、《せんだいメディアテーク》(2000)、《台中オペラハウス》(2015)などがある。

対話を終えて | After the conversation

僕は大学院生のときにラカトン&ヴァッサルの事務所で数カ月間インターンをした。当時はボルドーからパリに拠点を移したばかりのスタッフ数人の小さな事務所で、後に彼らの代表作となる《パレ・ド・トーキョー》の第1期工事（2001）の現場を進めていた。いまやスタッフ二十数名を抱える、フランスを代表する建築家である。現代の建築的課題に軽やかに立ち向かうその姿勢は、日本でも若い世代を中心に共感を呼んでいる。

対話は「より安いことは、より豊かなこと」であるという彼らのステートメントから始まった。「安いこと」とは、値段が「高いこと」の逆ではなく、建築の目的、つまりお金を「なんのために使うのか」を問い直すことだ、と言う。利用者に自由と可能性をもたらすために、同じ予算で2倍の床面積のプロジェクトにする。《ラタピ邸》から始まった誰でもわかるこの単純な方法論を、実際に住宅、公営の集合住宅、学校、美術館とさまざまなプログラムで、あるいは新築、増改築のプロジェクトで実現してきた。説得力は十分である。面積や窓の大きさなど「最小限」の規制から導かれる昨今の建築の貧しさを訴えていたことも印象的だった。彼らはプロジェクトの可能性を「最大限」に押し広げることに力を注ぐのだ。

歴史についての考え方もラカトン&ヴァッサルらしい。「私たちは、実際に自分で見て学ぶことが大事だと考えています」とヴァッサルが言うとおり、歴史を過去のものとせず今日を持続的につくりだしているものと捉え、旅や都市のリサーチで見聞したものを、好奇心をもって掘り下げていくプロセスを重視する。いわばプロジェクトごとに、その都度、今日から過去に向かって歴史を立ち上げていくような態度である。インプットとアウト

When I was a graduate student I worked as an intern at Lacaton & Vassal's office for several months. They had just moved their headquarters from Bordeaux to Paris, and it was a small office with just a few staffers. It was 2001 and they were working on-site during the first stage of reconstruction at the Palais de Tokyo, which would later become their best-known work. Today they are one of France's premier architect firms, with a staff of over twenty. The lighthearted, graceful manner with which they confront contemporary architectural issues resonates with Japanese architects, particularly those of the younger generation.

Our interview began with their declaration that "cheaper is more." By "cheaper" they do not mean the opposite of "expensive" in terms of price, but rather, a reevaluation of a building's purpose that asks what the money is being spent for. To afford the user more freedom and possibilities, they strive to double the space provided within a given budget. Starting with Latapie House, they have successfully applied this simple, clearcut methodology to all kinds of projects, from homes to public housing complexes to schools to museums, in structures both new and rebuilt. Their argument is quite persuasive. Also impressive is their critique of the impoverished nature of contemporary architecture that is born of restrictions that keep space, windows and so on to a minimum. In contrast they devote themselves to expanding the potential of their projects to the maximum.

Lacaton and Vassal also have their own distinctive take on history. As Vassal states, "What is important ... is to learn from what we see." History, as they view it, is not of the

プット、知識と実践をつねに一体化させるような彼らの「アイレベル」の歴史への眼差しがとても興味深かった。

　広いオフィスの隅に小さな部屋があった。そこにはワインの大量のストックが常備されていて（2人ともワインの名産地として知られるボルドー出身）、さらにヴァッサルの小さな植物実験室にもなっている。光や温湿度を管理し、世界中の植物を育てる実験を繰り返しているのだという。趣味だと言いながらも、彼は真剣である。もちろん建築プロジェクトへの展開も念頭に置いているそうだ。とても小さな部屋だったが、建築を真剣に楽しむこと、あるいはプラグマティックかつ理想主義的であることを求める2人の建築観がよく表われていると思った。

past, but continually creates the present. They place great value on applying their curiosity to what they observe in their travels and research on cities. You might say that for every project they embark on, they look from the present to the past and get history up and running for that project. I was fascinated by their "eye-level" view of history, which unifies input and output, knowledge and practice as one.

　In one corner of their spacious office was a small room. It contained a sizeable stock of wines (both of them are from Bordeaux, known for its wine), as well as a mini-lab for Vassal's experiments with plants. He says that he test-grows plants from all over the world under different conditions of light, temperature and humidity. Though he calls it a hobby, he is very serious about it. Naturally he also considers how to apply his findings to their architectural projects. It's a very small room, but it eloquently reflects the attitude both of them share toward architecture: dedicated enjoyment and a determination to be at once pragmatic and utopian.

Anne Lacaton & Jean-Philippe Vassal

ラタピ邸／ボルドー、フランス／1993
Latapie House/Bordeaux, France/1993

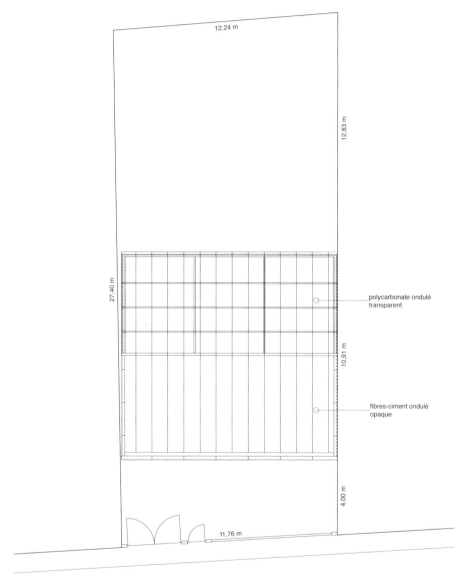

polycarbonate ondulé transparent

fibres-ciment ondulé opaque

rue du 8 MAI 45

配置図 1:200
site plan 1:200

Anne Lacaton & Jean-Philippe Vassal

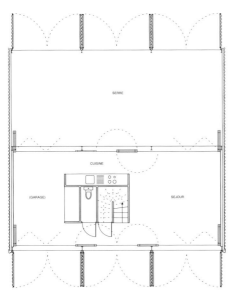

1階平面図 1:200
first floor plan 1:200

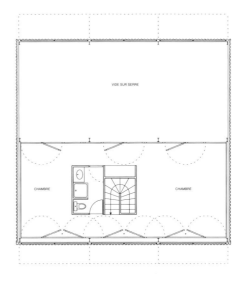

2階平面図 1:200
second floor plan 1:200

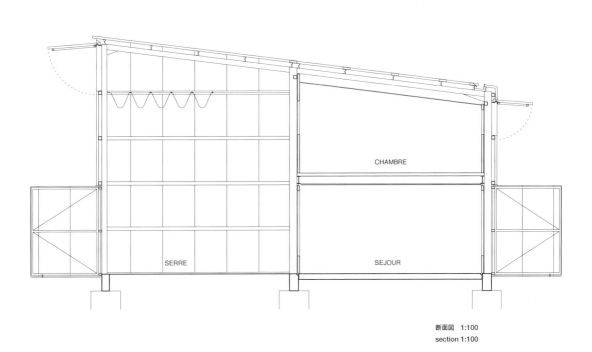

断面図 1:100
section 1:100

Anne Lacaton & Jean-Philippe Vassal

ラタピ邸
Latapie House

Anne Lacaton & Jean-Philippe Vassal

Anne Lacaton & Jean-Philippe Vassal

ラタピ邸
Latapie House

Anne Lacaton & Jean-Philippe Vassal

Anne Lacaton & Jean-Philippe Vassal

Bois-le-Prêtre Tower Block Transformation／Paris, France／2011

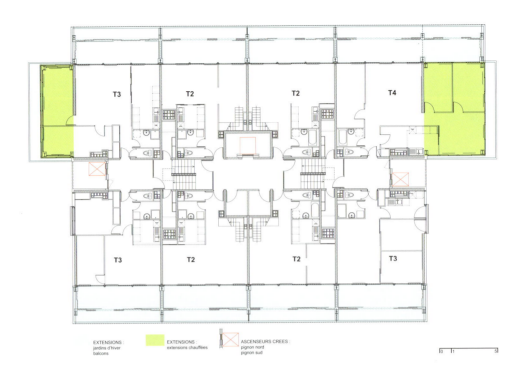

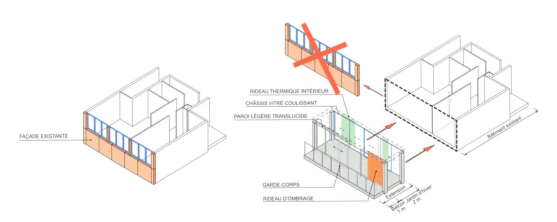

APPARTEMENT T2 EXISTANT APPARTEMENT T2 + EXTENSION (JARDIN D'HIVER 15 m2 + BALCON 7,5 m2)

Anne Lacaton & Jean-Philippe Vassal

Anne Lacaton & Jean-Philippe Vassal

ボワ・ル・プレートル高層住宅の改修
Bois-le-Prêtre Tower Block Transformation

Anne Lacaton & Jean-Philippe Vassal

Anne Lacaton & Jean-Philippe Vassal

Pascal Flammer

30th April 2014
@ House in Balsthal, Switzerland

Pascal Flammer

Three reasons to travel

Go Hasegawa   How did you get your start in architecture?

Pascal Flammer   I started off my bachelor studies at Swiss Federal Institute of Technology Lausanne (EPF Lausanne), then I went to Delft University of Technology (TU Delft) for a year. It was the time when all this powerful, but for us also cryptic, work from the Netherlands came over to Switzerland. We couldn't really read and understand it, but it seemed fresh and subversive—it was very attractive!

GH   In the 1990s.

PF   Yes. I wanted to see Dutch architecture and understand their topics and ways of production, but after a year I was not really happy. I had hoped there was more. So, because I had always been very interested in Sigurd Lewerentz, Alvar Aalto, and Kay Fisker[1], as well as the films of Aki Kaurismäki[2], I went on a long trip to Northern Europe. The Scandinavian approach seemed to be another way. They were very down to earth, those old masters, classical but also very curious and outrageous, searching for proposals very close to their bodies and brains: searching for a contemporaneity based on a classical foundation—and never schematic. There are beautiful landscapes and beautiful cities, like Stockholm. There is something very humanistic in those cities, as well as in the work of those old masters. It is somehow about life and the inevitability of death. I was deeply touched by that work, maybe mostly by Lewerentz, that heavy beauty. But I also felt that this work is finished—old, from the past. Beautiful and over, the architecture of our fathers. There was nothing formal or social to copy, or to continue to adapt to our time. Only the inhabited ability to express human existence. I learned how existential and touching architecture can be.

After three months of travelling in Scandinavia I had to leave. I didn't find a job to earn money and I knew I had to restart. After my return to Switzerland a friend took me to the office of Valerio Olgiati. That was the first time I met Valerio. I admired this man and his work, and some days later I was working in his office. It was quite small—there were just three of us—Valerio, a draftsman, and me. It was a fantastic and inspiring time, it was the first time architectural production made profound sense to me. Valerio was asked to be a guest professor at Swiss Federal Institute of Technology Zürich (ETH Zürich). So I went to study there under him for one more year and got my diploma.

GH   I see.

PF   With my diploma in hand, I wanted to go to Japan. This was my big dream. I was very interested in the architecture of Kazuo Shinohara and I had seen a lot of movies, both old and new, from and about Japan. I was fascinated about old as well as contemporary Japanese production. Japan was for me always a big projection surface, and yet I had no clue how one feels having one's feet in that country. After my studies I had no money but I really wanted to go, so with two friends we decided to drive there, in our Fiat Panda that was parked in front of our door! (laughs)

Well, that was quite a long trip. We drove through rather quickly to the western part of Turkey and from then on slowly and extensively through Lebanon, Syria, and Iran. Very beautiful! We would drive and visit in the day and at sunset we would stop wherever we were and pull the blankets out of the car. Quite often, farmers would come to us early in the morning, carrying a small silver tray with coffee, olives, water, and a bowl to wash our faces with. We talked a bit with these families, we shared no common language, but we would show photos and say where we were from, and they would show us their kids, wives, the kitchen, and so on. And then we would drive off again. When we arrived in Pakistan, to cross over into China, it was 9/11; the towers had fallen in New York. Our contact with the Swiss embassy advised us to come home quickly. As a consequence, our trip was aborted and we had to drive all that distance back. I didn't manage to get to Japan!

GH   That was a pity. But you travelled a lot when you were a student and I guess these trips were significant to you in many ways.

PF   Yes, absolutely. I spent a year in Australia and some time in California during secondary school. During my holidays in high school and university I always went abroad: Egypt, Israel, Maghreb, Western and Eastern Europe, the USA, Thailand, three times to India, China... Well, there are manifolds of meanings. The first is maybe simply to leave the known for the unknown. It gives you a very strong feeling of your own presence. The climate is different and people and things in your surroundings act and react in a different way than you are used to. Second, simply to see what other cultures and periods have made and do. And the third has to do with relativity: by encountering beliefs and dogmas different to your own, you realize how relative values are. This is a nice feeling, it provides distance and calm. What remains is yourself trying to give sense and value to your surroundings. That is what I actually try to do as an architect.

I returned through Iran and then back to Switzerland, where Valerio asked me to work again in his office, which I did—from 2001 to 2005.

GH   How was your experience there?

PF   During my studies, I understood architecture as a kind of game where you somehow have to answer the professors' requests. It was at Valerio's office where I first became interested in architecture as a physical extension of its creator. Architecture is not just a response to someone's wanting something. I started to see that architecture is an interpretation of your understanding of the world. Or a means by which you try to establish an understanding of the world. Your design is based on that understanding, and yet the building itself also shows a way through which you can deepen your understanding. This is the core of what I learned at Valerio's office, and what I brought to my own work.

Control vs. the uncontrolled

PF   After leaving Valerio's office I went to São Paulo, to see the architecture of Paulo Mendes da Rocha[3] and Vilanova Artigas[4], two architects next to Shinohara whom I admire very much [fig.1]. Of course there is the entire Paulista school[5] as well as some Carioca school[6], and I was attracted to the climate as well. I liked the idea of living in a hot place because I was used to a cold city. There was this immediate meeting or clash of jungle and concrete.

While in Brazil I got my first commission for a favela project[7] in Rio de Janeiro, a community center for local people (Centro Comunitário Júlio Otoni, 2005) [fig.2, 3]. It had too large a program for the size of the site, and little money. Therefore, I proposed a concrete piloti structure where the floor plates grow in size with each floor. It had small spans and no glass. All facades were covered with movable wood panels that were nicely protected from the rain by the floor plate above. The entire building was one large stapled public space—a mini Centre Pompidou (1977) in a favela that is very short on public space, as all non-occupied space is immediately taken over by private dwellers. At one point the promoter stopped responding. I was told he got shot! The project then came to a standstill, unfortunately.

GH   Wow. How terrible! For the project, as well. That would've been a nice building if completed.

Let's talk about this House in Balsthal (2012) [fig.4]. I like this room we're in now very much. On this semi-underground level I can sense the outside as being very close. We're at the same eye level with tulips and small animals on the field. It's refreshing to feel on such even ground with nature. Probably from this room we are able to sense nature much more closely than if we were actually standing outside.

What would you say about the relationship between this space and upstairs, with its high ceiling?

PF   I juxtapose two very different spaces. Both spaces are dependent on each other in the sense that each space reveals the quality of the other. If you are down here, on the ground floor, you experience a specific emotion. Then, when you go upstairs, you experience yet a very different sensation. What remains is the viewer, the observer—the curiosity of a seeking mind. In the end this house is about the person who visits it. In other words, by the means of space the building is about man and not about space itself. The space is simply a tool to question or reframe your own existence.

GH   That's very interesting.

PF   With that said, there is a difference between the two spaces. I think of the ground floor as an animalistic space. That comes from being somehow afraid because you are exposed and can't hide here in this fully glazed space next to an unknown forest. Yet at the same time you are protected by the ground, since the house is lowered 750 millimeters into the earth. I would say these reactions lie at a pre-cognitive level, before you think—a kind of a psychological moment. Such feelings are simple, very primitive ones, but that is also why they are strong. It is a space where you have little control—you are just a part of the surrounding landscape.

The upper floor is the opposite. It is a space where you are in the center. It is a walled room, six meters high, with framed openings. In principle it's a space where the individual is in the middle and looks at a painting, or at the landscape. There is a vis-à-vis relation between the viewer and the landscape he observes, a dynamic of control. Also, the upper space is fully artificial: a rectangle divided by two walls into four equal spaces, twice a division of a rectangle through its middle axis. It is the most direct way to divide a space, like an army general would do. As a consequence you have four times the same space and you reach these not through a corridor, but by walking straight from one to the next, like an enfilade, or, more precisely, as in Villa La Rotonda (1567-70) [fig.5].

So we have landscape vs. manmade space. The question of the center is very important: upstairs the visitor is the center; on the ground floor there is no center, there is just universe. Or one could also say the building is about control vs. the arbitrary and uncontrolled. All elements of the ground floor—the position of the pillars and stairs for example—are a result of strategic decisions made for the upper floor, but they are spatially senseless on the ground floor—they are just "somewhere."

Double or parallel existence

GH Your works are abstract, yet concrete. On the one hand, this building is schematic and clear, and yet the space is welcoming to a normal life with a normal chair, for example. It is not merely extreme. Take the pine panels. Pine is a cozy and rather sweet material, but when you notice that all of the surfaces—floor, wall, and ceiling—are composed solely of pine, the impression is no longer just sweet. The singularity of material lends a kind of abstraction even as it has materiality. And I like the dry joints between the pine panels; this detail works well.

PF I would like to make buildings that don't have any agenda other than the visitor and the cosmos. In order to achieve this, nothing should be predominant, nothing should be topical. But at the same time the construction should give a feeling of presence to the person inside. In order to achieve presence some aspects must be extreme. In this house that would be for example the structure of the building—the fact that the entire building is made of only one material and of course its relation to the outside, and maybe also the heights of the inside spaces. It is a kind of contradiction: these aspects must on the one hand be very present, so one feels as though he were entering a special zone, but at the same time these aspects must also fall away, so that one does not think about them. A good building should not indicate anything; it should simply activate the inhabitant. As a consequence I have to find the balance between the abstract, concrete, schematic, and un-schematic. The building should have no hierarchy—a silent presence. The best would be a building where you restart your thinking as a person, not questions about society or structure. And I don't mean in a negative way, but in a neutral or positive way. A good building or any good creation brings one's own existence to the fore, makes it visible.

GH What do you have to say about "image" in a building? For example, from this house, I retain several images in my mind, such as the pine paneling, the round window, and the proportions of the gable roof. You also show the plan and section of House in Liguria (2014) [fig.6-9] overlaid on an oil painting. I sense your interest in images.

PF   I use images as a tool, as I would use structure or abstraction as a tool in order to produce presence. The image in itself has no meaning, neither as memory, nor as a sort of academic or popular continuity of history. The gabled roof in Balsthal makes the house look like a typical countryside house of the area. I do that not because I find it important that it looks homogenous or analogous to the site per se—rather, I do that because it's the expression that doesn't make you think anything. The way this house looks is of zero importance and since you must give every house a form, I chose the one that has the lowest expression—a form that looks unspecific and generic to this region: the large gabled roof.

The graphic representation of the Liguria house—the plans with some painted girls below—is a bit less clear to me what it does. I made those plans when I was working with a phenomenon that I would like to call "double or parallel existence." Music, painting, architecture, they are all able to do a beautiful thing that language—or at least my skills in language—does less well: making two things at the same time, without any hierarchy. In music we can have two parallel, yet different, melodies. Language or logic on the other hand is singular: one thesis leads to a next. But a double (or multiple) presence of things accords to our daily experience. So I tried to do this double presence with an architectural plan: a random classical oil painting of a woman and a plan of a house. As in music, you can read both presences singularly and independently, or in parallel. This sounds conceptual and schematic, but in reality I tried many different backgrounds and in the end I chose a specific one because I thought it fits best of all those I tested. As a consequence one could say it is conceptual as well as it is composed.

A liberating cannibalism

PF   I think the generation before me, who are my teachers—contemporaries of Valerio Olgiati and Christian Kerez[8], for example, and maybe even one generation before, such as Herzog & de Meuron[9]—started their work with a different set of conditions. The question of whether to take images or abstract inventions as reference—in other words, the question to be Postmodernistic vs. Modernistic—seems to me a principal struggle in, but also a key source of invention for, their work. It seems that generation was constantly wrestling with this topic, at least at the start of their architectural production. I have the impression that my generation is different, this energy doesn't exist anymore. We are used to a world or system that has no strong part that you have to fight for or against. We have no enemy. We build up from neutral ground. Our work is not a reaction to something.

GH   Valerio recently said, "I don't believe in anything."

PF   I believe everything. But, I guess Valerio's statement shows the fight with all kind of dogmas that this generation was confronted with. Valerio comes to the conclusion that he wants to, or does, reject them all. It also seems to me that this question of belief—not in a religious understanding, but more in the sense of the German expression "Haltung," which is about what you stand for, your dogmas, what side you take—is a very European topic. I think it is very reactive. Here in Europe it is the key to define yourself and is central to our relations with others. But I have the impression it is the condition of the "old world." It reminds me of the Brazilian concept, something I'm quite fascinated by.

GH   The Brazilian concept?

PF   The concept of cannibalism. It's a proposal that goes back to the 1930s, suggesting how the Brazilians were able to assimilate or eat up the incoming European concepts instead of reacting to them. For example, Le Corbusier's ideas. They ate them to their own taste, in the way they wanted. They manipulated them according to their social, economical, and climatic reality. No big fuss.

   For me this is an interesting way to see such migration of ideas. I find it very inspiring. It's direct, cruel, dirty, and dangerous, because it could lead to good results but also to bad. The difficulty is that there is no critical position and it is hard to foresee the consequences, but that is also its beauty—it's pure and striving to change things quickly for the better. It's the expression of a community that sees a program for its future. I find this a very liberating way to give birth to something new, and I wish Europe had more of this power even though it is as intellectual as a rock band. (Laughs)

GH   That is so interesting. I too feel I don't share the same values as the generation before me. For them, overcoming something was the main topic of their architecture. But we build our architecture from neutral ground, as you said.

PF   Once I asked you a very simple question: "What are your topics?" And you answered, "Proportions. It's all I do. What is the relation between the things, what is the relation to outside, where is this building in the ground? Is it light, is it heavy, is it high, is it low?" I find this answer to be very liberating. It doesn't answer the question we are talking about now directly, but there is still a lot there to go on. That topic touches on everything: land, construction, man, city, and scale. So I find this a very elegant way to avoid entering this dilemma of being Modernist or not.

GH   I want to think about what's possible with an architecture that can deal with a myriad of topics. Certainly it's easy to understand reactive architecture that focuses on social issues or current trends. But I question how long such work will endure. Álvaro Siza also told me about the importance of multiplicity in architecture.

Historical maturity

PF   I would be interested to know more about the Japanese way. Do the Japanese have this similar dilemma? For a European, this hybrid condition in Japan is fascinating. Things are new and at the same time very old, and in a strange way unphysical, as if it were only a temporary proposal. Like Ise Shrine, for example—the fact that it is an old place that is rebuilt periodically. So, beyond its symbolic value, this place is not just a museum for old craftsmanship. And then there is this accidental city of Tokyo, where everything is somehow new. What does it mean for architects?

GH   As far as architecture is concerned, I think that for some time, presenting one new thing after another has taken priority over any discussion of history or older Japanese culture.

One thing that surprises me at the Academy of Architecture in Mendrisio is that the students often show me a sort of reference like a villa in Italy. I worry that this is a bit conservative, a stereotype. But sometimes it's very fresh for me to see a project that reveals both the contemporary and historical sense that young European students have. I find a sort of historical maturity there.

But Japanese people do tend to react to the current situation, and forget it soon. It is a bit like consumption. What is the hot topic now? Who is the next one? How will architecture respond? Certainly it's important to understand what's happening now, but at the same time I think architecture should not be so simplistic. Maybe this happens because of the short sense of historical scale in architecture in Japan.

But since the 2011 earthquake, Japanese society and architects have started to think and talk a lot more about time and history. This is a big change. Actually it is this very situation in Japan that motivated me to come and speak with European architects.

1 —— Kay Fisker: Danish architect born in 1893 and deceased in 1965. While advocating for functionalism, his works on the other hand are characterized by traditional design based on Scandinavian brickwork. He designed many residences in Copenhagen. One of his pupils was Arne Jacobsen.
2 —— Aki Kaurismäki: Finnish film director born in 1957. Best known for "Crime and Punishment" (1983) and "The Man Without a Past" (2002).
3 —— Paulo Mendes da Rocha: Brazilian architect born in 1928. Major projects include "Club Athletico Paulistano" (1957)

and "Chapel of Saint Peter" (1987). Received the Pritzker Prize in 2006.

4 —— Vilanova Artigas: Brazilian Modernist architect born in 1915 and deceased in 1985. Major works include "Artigas House" (1949) and "Faculty of Architecture and Urban Planning Center at University São Paulo" (1969).

5 —— Paulista school: Group of São Paulo architects formed in the 1950s, among them Paulo Mendes da Rocha.

6 —— Carioca school: Group of Rio de Janeiro architects. A key figure was Oscar Niemeyer (1902-2012).

7 —— Favela projects: Favelas are slum areas in which makeshift shanties are built within suburbs and big cities in Brazil. There was a failed campaign to remove the settlements in 1960. Learning from the failures of that movement, favela projects after 2000 seek to guarantee the welfare of inhabitants by offering employment support and constructing roads, water, and sewage infrastructures.

8 —— Christian Kerez: Architect working in Switzerland originally from Venezuela, born in 1962. Major commissions include "Oberrealta Chapel" (1992) and "Leutschenbach School" (2009).

9 —— Herzog & de Meuron: Architectural office established in late 1970's by two architects, Jacques Herzog and Pierre de Meuron (both of Swiss origin born in 1950). Widely known for many works specializing in designs for external skins, such as Signal Box (1994) and Prada Boutique Aoyama (2003).

パスカル・フラマー

2014年4月30日
スイス、《バルシュタールの住宅》にて

旅に出る3つの理由

長谷川豪（以下、GH）　ではまず、建築の道を歩みはじめてからの経緯を教えてください。

パスカル・フラマー（以下、PF）　スイス連邦工科大学ローザンヌ校（EPF Lausanne）で建築を学び、卒業後、デルフト工科大学（TU Delft）でさらに1年間、勉強をしました。その頃はオランダの建築が業界を席巻しており、われわれにとっては神秘的な作品群がスイスで紹介されはじめた時期でした。すぐには理解できないようなものばかりでしたが、どれも斬新で破壊的に見えたし、とにかく魅力的でした。

GH　90年代のことですね。

PF　そうです。私はオランダの建築を理解したかったし、彼らがどんな思想を持っていて、どんな方法で設計をしているのかを知りたかったのです。でも1年くらい経つと当初の興奮は徐々に冷めていきました。もっといろいろ発見できると期待していたのですが。そして、私は北欧への長い旅に出ることにしたのです。シーグルド・レヴェレンツ、アルヴァ・アールト、ケイ・フィスカー[1]、映画監督のアキ・カウリスマキ[2]といった人物にずっと興味を持っていたこともあります。スカンジナビアの方法論はオランダのものとはまったく別のものでした。巨匠たちの作品は、地に足がついていて、古典的でありながらとんでもなく刺激的で、身体や脳に働きかけてきました。古典的な原理につながりながらも現代の感覚に訴えかけてく

るものであり、オランダの図式的な建築とは違っていました。私はストックホルムのような美しいランドスケープや都市に巡り会いました。北欧の都市は人間味にあふれ、また巨匠たちの作品群もそのなかに位置づけられているのです。そこには生きることと、そして人として避けることのできない死というものに通じるなにかがあると感じました。なかでもレヴェレンツの重厚で美しい作品に対して心を大きく動かされました。それと同時に、その作品は完成されたもの、歳をとっていて、過去のものであると感じました。美しいのですが、すでに終わってしまったもの、言ってみれば父親たちによる建築です。形態的にも社会的にも私たちの時代に応用できるような真似すべきものはないという印象を持ちました。そこは、人間の存在を示すための居住性があるだけです。建築が人間の存在にかかわるもので、また感動的なものであるということは感じとることができました。

3カ月ほどして、私はスカンジナビアの旅を終えなければならなくなりました。お金が底をつきましたが仕事も見つからず、再スタートを切らなければならなかったのです。スイスに戻るとすぐに、友人がヴァレリオ・オルジャティの事務所に連れていってくれました。そこでヴァレリオにはじめて会いました。私は彼の人柄と作品に感銘を受けました。そして数日後には、私は彼の事務所で働いていました。当時はまだとても小さな事務所で、ヴァレリオ、製図スタッフ、そして私の3人だけでした。素晴らしく、刺激的な日々でした。建築を創造するという行為がはじめてとても深遠なものに思えたのです。その頃、ヴァレリオはスイス連邦工科大学チューリッヒ校（ETH Zürich）の客員教授として学生を指導していました。私は1年間、彼の下で学び、学位を取ったのです。

GH　そうだったんですか。

PF　学位を取得した後、私は日本に行こうと考えました。それは私の大きな夢でした。私は篠原一男の建築にとても興味を持っていたし、日本映画も古いものから新しいものまでたくさん見てきました。日本の伝統だけでなく、現代的な作品にも感銘を受けました。私にとって日本はいつも大きなスクリーンのようなものだったので実際に足を踏み入れたときにどう感じるのか、なかなか想像できませんでした。大学院で勉強した後でお金がなかったのですが、どうしても日本に行きたかったので、2人の友人と日本に向けて車で行ってみようと決めて、外に停めてあるフィアット・パンダで出発したんです！（笑）

長い長い旅でした。トルコ西部を比較的短い日数で走り抜けて、その先にあるレバノン、シリア、イランといった地域を時間をかけて移動しました。とても美しい風

景でした。太陽が出ているあいだに移動し、いろいろな場所を訪れました。太陽が沈む頃に車からブランケットを引っ張り出して眠りました。農家の近くで眠ったときなどは、朝になると農家の人たちがシルバーの小さなトレーにコーヒー、オリーブ、飲み水、そして顔を洗うための洗面器を持ってきてくれたこともありました。農家の家族とのちょっとした会話も楽しみました。共通する言語はありませんでしたが、私たちは写真を見せながらどこから来たのかを話し、農夫は子どもたちや奥さんを紹介してくれて、炊事場を見せてくれたこともあります。そして再び移動するということを繰り返しました。中国への国境を越えるためパキスタンに到着したとき、ちょうど9.11のテロが起き、ニューヨークのビルが崩壊しました。そしてスイス大使館から至急、帰国するようにと通達がありました。その結果、私たちは旅を止めてそれまで移動してきた道を引き返すことになったのです。結局、日本にはたどり着けませんでした。

GH　それは残念でしたね。でも若いときにたくさん旅をしたことはあなたにいろいろな影響を与えたのではないですか。

PF　そうです。中学生のときにはオーストラリアに1年間住んでいました。カリフォルニアに住んでいたこともあります。高校時代や大学時代は長い休みになるといつも外国に出かけました。エジプト、イスラエル、マグレブ、ヨーロッパの東部や西部、アメリカ、タイ。インドと中国には3回も行きました。旅にはいくつか意味があります。第一に、慣れ親しんだところから離れるということ。そうするとあなた自身の存在を強く感じることができます。気候も違うし、慣れ親しんだ環境とは違うやり方で人々も物事も反応してきます。第二に、ほかの文化や時代がどんなものを生み出し、そこでなにが起こっているのかを知ることができます。第三に——これは相対的なものですが——あなた自身のものとは異なる信仰や教義に出会うことがあります。あなたの価値観がいかに相対的なものかを知ることができるでしょう。それはとても新鮮な感覚です。客観性や落ち着きが得られます。残るのはあなたの周りの環境に意味や価値をもたらそうとするあなた自身です。それは私が建築家として目指していることそのものでもあります。

　私はイランを経由してスイスに戻りました。そのときヴァレリオが、また自分の事務所で働いてみないかと誘ってくれました。そして私は2001年から2005年まで彼の事務所で働いたのです。

GH　そこでの経験はどのようなものでしたか？

fig.1 パウロ・メンデス・ダ・ロシャ《サンペドロ教会》(1987)
Paulo Mendes da Rocha, Capela São Pedro Apóstolo, 1987

PF 大学で勉強していたとき、建築とは教授が出す要求にいかに応えるかというゲームのようなものだと捉えていました。けれどもヴァレリオの事務所で仕事をしているときに、私ははじめて建築がそれを生み出す者の物理的な延長なのではないかと思うようになりました。建築は誰かの欲求に応えるだけではないのです。それは自分が世界をどう理解しているかということに深くかかわるものなのではないかと考えるようになりました。もしくは建築は世界に対する理解を確立していくことなのではないかと。デザインはその理解に基づいており、建物は自分自身の理解をより深める道筋を示しているのです。それは私がヴァレリオの事務所で学んだ最も重要なことで、私自身の仕事の核心にもなっています。

　ヴァレリオの事務所を離れてから、私はサンパウロに行きました。パウロ・メンデス・ダ・ロシャ[3]とヴィラノヴァ・アルティガス[4]の建築を見に行ったのです[fig.1]。篠原に次いで私がとても尊敬する建築家たちです。もちろんそこにはサンパウロ派[5]の作品群が揃っており、カリオカ派[6]の作品もいくつか見ることができました。私は現地の気候にも魅了されました。涼しい都市に暮らすことに慣れすぎたせいか、私はこの蒸し暑い土地が気に入ったのです。森林とコンクリートの唐突な出会いも衝撃的でした。ブラジルで、私はリオ・デ・ジャネイロで最初のファヴェーラ・プロジェクト[7]を設計する機会を得ました。地元の人々のためのコミュニティ・センターを建てるというものです(《フリオ・オトニのコミュニティ・センター》2005) [fig.2, 3]。敷地や予算の規模に対してプログラムの要求は過剰なものでし

fig.2　フリオ・オトニのコミュニティ・センター（2005）
Centro Comunitário Júlio Otoni, 2005

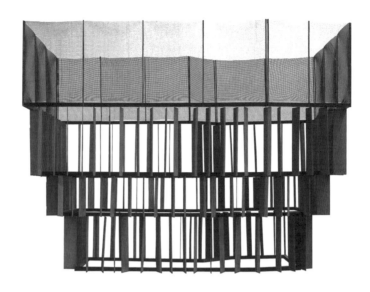

た。そこで私はコンクリート構造のピロティで、上階にいくにしたがって床面積が大きくなるような建築を提案しました。構造のスパンは小さく、ガラスは使っていません。ファサードはすべて可動式の木製パネルで覆われており、それらは上階の床の張り出しによって雨から守られるようになっています。建物全体が積層されたひとつの大きなパブリック・スペースになっています。占有されていない空間があればすぐに私有化されてしまうため、パブリック・スペースが極端に少ないファヴェーラにおける極小版《ポンピドゥ・センター》(1977)のようなものとして構想したのですが、あるときプロモーターから返事が来なくなりました。どうやら射殺されたらしいというのです。それ以来、プロジェクトも止まってしまいました。

GH　それは残念でしたね。完成していたらとてもよい建物になっていたと思います。

コントロールすること vs. コントロールしないこと

GH　この住宅《バルシュタールの住宅》(2012) [fig.4]について話をしましょう。いま私たちがいる部屋はとても気持ちがいいですね。半地下になっているこの部屋からは外部がとても近く感じられます。私たちの目線が、チューリップや庭にいる小さな動物たちと同じ高さにあって、こんなふうに自然の地面を感じられるのはとても新鮮です。もしかしたら外に立っているよりも、この室内にいるときのほうが自然

fig.3 フリオ・オトニのコミュニティ・センター
Centro Comunitário Júlio Otoni

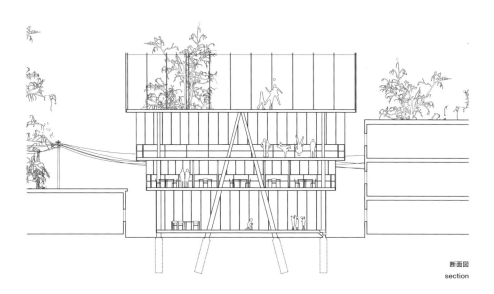

断面図
section

を身近に感じるのではないでしょうか。この半地下の空間と上階にある天井の高い空間の関係についてはどのように考えていたのですか？

PF　私は2つの対比的な空間を並置しました。2つの空間は、それぞれがもう一方の特性を強調するという意味で互いに補完し合う関係にあります。下の地階にいるとなにか特別な感覚が得られます。そして上の階にいくと、また別な感覚が得られると思います。異なる2つの状態のあいだで変わらずに残るのは見る人、観察者であり、なにかを探求しようとする好奇心です。この住宅はここを訪れる人に働きかけようとしています。言い換えると、この建物は空間そのものではなく人にかかわる探求の場なのです。空間は、あなたという存在を問う、あるいは見つめ直すための道具と言えるかもしれません。

GH　面白いですね。

PF　2つの空間のあいだには差異を定義できます。1階は動物的な空間と言えるでしょう。あなたは得体のしれない森のような場所にさらけ出されていて、身を隠すことができないため、ある種の恐怖を覚えると思います。と同時に、あなたは地面により守られている。床面が地表面から750mmほど低く掘り下げられています。あなたの反応は知覚以前のもの、考える以前のもので、心理的な反応と言えるものです。この感覚は単純で、原始的なものですが、それゆえに強いものです。このよ

fig.4　バルシュタールの住宅 (2012)
House in Balthal, 2012

Pascal Flammer

Pascal Flammer

fig.5 アンドレア・パッラーディオ《ヴィラ・ロトンダ》(1567–70)
Andrea Palladio, Villa La Rotonda, 1567-70

　うな空間であなたは自分をコントロールすることができません。むしろあなたは外の風景の一部にすぎないのです。

　上の階はまったく正反対です。その空間ではあなたが中心にいます。周りはすべて6mの高い壁で囲まれており、開口部は縁取られています。基本的には個人が中心にいて、絵画や風景を眺めるようになっています。観察者と観察される風景は「見る–見られる(vis-à-vis)」という関係にあり、その関係はダイナミックにコントロールされます。上階の空間はとても人工的です。長方形が2つの壁によって4つの同じような空間に分割されています。ひとつの空間を、軍隊の司令官がやるように直截的に、2つの空間に分割しています。その結果、同じ空間を4回経験することになります。それも廊下を挟むことなく、アンフィラード（続き部屋）——より正確にはアンドレア・パッラーディオ《ヴィラ・ロトンダ》(1567–70) [fig.5]——のようにひとつの空間から次の空間へ直接、移動するのです。

　つまりランドスケープと人工的な空間が対置されているというわけです。中心性に関する問いはとても重要です。上階では人間が中心にいて、下階では中心がなく、ただ世界だけがあります。この建物は、コントロールするものとコントロールできないものの対比であると言うこともできます。下階のすべてのエレメント、例えば柱や階段といったものは、上階における意思決定の結果ですが、でもそのことは下階では空間的に意味をなしていません。ただそこに存在しているだけです。

Pascal Flammer

二重性、あるいは並行的存在

GH あなたの作品には抽象性があります。でもそこには確かな存在感もあります。建物は図式的で明快です。でも空間は普通の生活、普通の家具を受け入れる寛容さを持っており、極端なものではありません。例えばパイン材のパネル。パインは親しみやすくて温かみのある素材です。でも床、壁、天井とすべての表面がパイン材で統一された仕上げになっていると単なる温かみ以上のものを感じます。ひとつの素材に統一することで素材感とは異なる、空間の抽象性が出現しています。パインのパネル同士のジョイントは空目地になっていて、このディテールも効いていますね。

PF 私はそこを訪れる人やそこにある世界のあり方を問題にするような建物をつくりたいと思っています。そのためには、卓越したものや主張のようなものがあってはいけません。その一方で、建物はそのなかにいる人に対して即物的に語りかけなくてはなりません。即物的に語りかけるためには、ある要素を極端化する必要があります。この住宅において、それは建物の構造体ということになると思います。例えば、建物全体が単一のマテリアルでできていること、外部との関係、そして内部空間の高さが挙げられます。ある意味では矛盾するかもしれませんが、素材や気積といった性質は実体的なもので、人が特別な領域に身を置いていることを体感させます。その一方で、それらの性質ははがれ落ち、人はそれらをあまり意識することはありません。いい建物はなにも主張すべきではなく、ささやかに居住者の暮らしを豊かにすべきなのです。だから私は抽象性、実体性、図式的なもの、図式的でないもののバランスをとるようにしています。建物はヒエラルキーを持つことなく、ささやかな存在であるべきです。理想的なのは、われわれがひとりの人間であるということを再確認できるような建物で、社会やシステム的なことといったものを問うことではないのです。私は否定的にではなく、中立的で前向きに考えようとしています。優れた建物、あるいは優れた創造行為とは、人の存在に光を当て、それを考えさせるものだと思っています。

GH 建物の「イメージ」についてはどのように考えていますか？　例えば、この住宅からは、パイン材のパネル、丸窓、そして切り妻屋根などいくつかのイメージが頭のなかに残ります。また、例えばあなたは油絵の上に「リグーリアの住宅」（2009–）の平面図や断面図をオーバーレイするという独特の表現も行なっていますね [fig.6-9]。こうしたイメージに、なにか特別な関心があるように思うのですが。

fig.6, 7 「リグーリアの住宅」(2009 −)
House in Liguria, 2009-

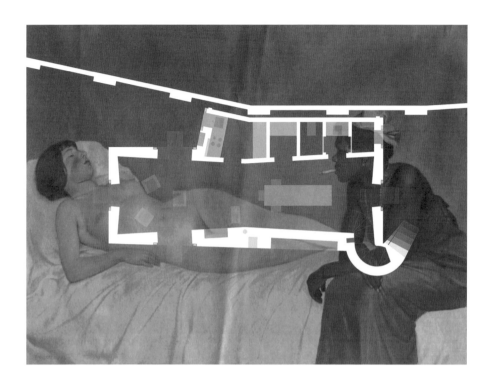

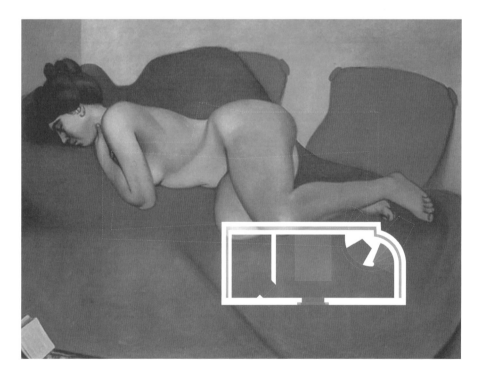

Pascal Flammer

fig.8, 9 「リグーリアの住宅」
House in Liguria

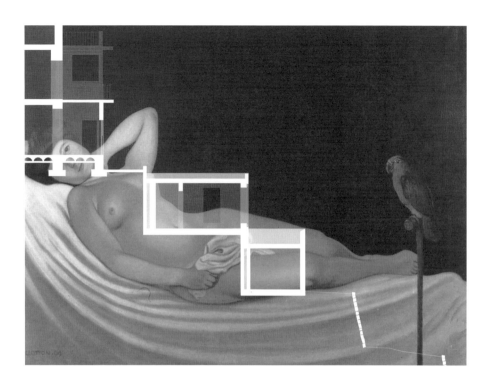

Pascal Flammer

PF イメージはツールとして使っています。存在感をつくりだすために構造や抽象性をツールとして使うのと同じです。イメージは、記憶でもなく、学術的あるいは大衆的な歴史の連続性でもなく、それ自体に意味はありません。《バルシュタールの住宅》の切り妻屋根は、それが建つ地域に見られる典型的な民家を連想させます。そのような形にしたのは敷地の周りにある民家の形状に合わせたり、それらに似たものにするためというよりは、余計な連想を起こさせないためです。この住宅がどのように見えるかはまったく重要ではないのです。住宅を設計すれば、いずれそれに形を与えなくてはなりませんが、この地域において特別ではなく一般的に見えるものとして、最小限の表現として、大きな切り妻屋根を選択したのです。

「リグーリアの住宅」のグラフィック表現で、平面図の下に少女の絵を敷いたものがありますが、それがなにをもたらしているのか、私にはまだよくわかっていません。これらの平面図表現は、私が「二重性、あるいは並行的存在」と呼ぶ現象について考えていたときに作成しました。音楽、絵画、建築は、いずれも言語の(少なくとも私の言語能力の)限界を超えたなにかを成し遂げることができます。2つのことを、ヒエラルキーなしに共存させることができるのです。音楽では2つの併走する、それぞれに異なるメロディの共存が可能です。これに対して言語や論理には、ひとつの言説が次の言説へと続くといったように、ひとつの流れだけが存在します。2つのもの(あるいは複数のもの)が同時に存在するということはわれわれの日常的な体験に近い感覚です。だから私は建築の平面図の重ね合わせをやってみたのです。女性を描いた油絵を恣意的に選び、住宅の平面図と重ねてみました。音楽では、旋律をひとつのまとまった流れとしてもほかのものとは切り離された流れとしても理解できるし、なにかと併走する流れとしても理解できます。概念的で形式的な話に聞こえるかもしれませんね。でも平面図の背景に置くべきものとして、いくつかの絵画を具体的に試してみた結果、これしかないというものを選んだのです。だからコンセプチュアルであると同時に構成的、具体的でもあるのです。

開かれたカニバリズム

PF 私より上の世代の建築家たち、私の先生にあたる人たち、例えばヴァレリオ・オルジャティやクリスチャン・ケレツ[8]、もしかしたらヘルツォーク&ド・ムロン[9]のようなさらに上の世代の建築家たちは、私たちとは異なる条件下でデザインをはじめたのだと思います。イメージや抽象的なアイデアを参照するかどうか、言い換えるとポストモダニズムかモダニズムかということが、彼らの作品において大き

な問いであり課題だったように思います。彼らの世代はつねに、あるいは少なくともデザインをはじめるときには、この問題に向き合ってきたように思います。私たちの世代は違うでしょう。そのようなことに対する情熱はもう存在しません。私たちはもう、戦いを挑み、反抗すべき強い相手を失なった世界にいます。もう戦うべき相手はいないのです。中立的なところからはじめるのです。われわれの仕事はなにかに対する異議申し立てではないのです。

GH　先日会ったときヴァレリオは「私はなにも信じない」と言っていました。

PF　私はあらゆることを信じています。でも、ヴァレリオのその発言は、彼の世代を支えてきたあらゆる原理を問い直す態度なのだと思います。ヴァレリオは、それらをすべて否定するという結論に達したのでしょう。信じるものの有無に対する問いは、宗教的な考えではなく、ドイツにおける「態度（Haltung）」という考え方に通じるもので、あなたの立ち位置、教義、立場といったヨーロッパ的な考えだと思います。それはとても反抗的なものです。ヨーロッパでは、あなた自身の位置づけ、他者との関係性がとても重要です。でもそれは「古い世界」の話に思えます。そして私は、ブラジル的な思想にとても興味を惹かれています。

GH　ブラジル的思想ですか？

PF　カニバリズムの思想です。1930年頃に遡りますが、ブラジル人たちは当時流入してきたヨーロッパ的な思想を撥ねつけるのではなく、うまく飲み込み、食べつくしました。例えばル・コルビュジエの思想です。ブラジルではその思想を自分たちが望むように、独自の解釈で調理しました。彼らの社会的、経済的、そして気候的なリアリティに合わせて加工されたのです。特に大きな騒ぎにもならなかった。

　そのような思想の移植はとても興味深いものです。想像力を刺激されます。直接的で、冷淡で、土着的ですし、良い結果をもたらすこともあれば悪い結果をもたらすこともあるという意味では危険でもあります。そして適切な判断を下すための評価軸がないという意味では難しいことです。結果も予想できません。でもある状況を手っ取り早く、良い方向に変革したいという純粋な情熱のかたちでもあります。未来に向けてアクションを起こそうとコミュニティがとった表現なのです。なにか新しいものを生みだそうとするための開かれた方法といえるでしょう。ヨーロッパもあんなふうにパワーを解放できるといいですね、まあロックバンドのような頭でっかちもいいのですが（笑）。

GH　カニバリスムですか、とても面白いですね。私も、私より上の世代と価値観を共有していないところがあるように思います。彼らはなにかを乗り越えることを主題に置いて建築をつくっていましたが、あなたが話されたように私も中立的なところから建築をはじめます。

PF　以前、私はあなたに「あなたの主題はなんですか？」というシンプルな問いを投げかけました。あなたは「プロポーション、それだけです。モノとモノの関係性、室内と外部の関係性、地面に対してどう建つか。軽いのか、重いのか、高いのか、低いのかといったことです」と答えましたね。私は、あなたの主題はとても開かれていると思いました。それは私たちがたったいま議論していることと直接関係しないかもしれませんが、そこには議論すべきこと、探求すべきことがまだまだあります。あなたの主題はあらゆることに関係していますね。大地、建物、人間、都市、そしてスケール。モダニストかそうでないかというジレンマに陥らない、エレガントな道が開けていると思います。

GH　私はより多様な問題と対峙するために建築になにが可能かを考えたいのです。社会問題や、流行の話題にのみ焦点を当ててリアクションするような建築はわかりやすいのですが、それがどれくらいの時間に耐えうるかを考えるとやはり疑問を感じてしまいます。アルヴァロ・シザも、建築の多重性の大切さを話していました。

歴史観の成熟

PF　私は日本的な考え方に興味を持っています。日本人は私たちと同じようなジレンマを抱えているのでしょうか？　ヨーロッパから見れば、日本のハイブリッドな状況はとても魅力的なのです。新しいものがある一方で、伝統的なものもある。不思議と非物質的で、儚いもののようです。伊勢神宮は、古代から続く古い場所なのに、定期的に更新されています。その意味で伊勢神宮は、象徴的な価値を持つだけでなく、また伝統建築の博物館でもないのです。そして一方で、日本には最新のもので埋め尽くされた東京のような衝撃的な都市がある。こうしたことを日本の建築家たちはどう受け止めているのでしょうか？

GH　建築について言えば、日本文化の古いものや歴史について語ることよりも、新しいものを次々に提示することのほうが、しばらく優先されてきたように思います。

メンドリシオ建築アカデミーで私が驚いたのは、学生たちがよくイタリアの古い民家を参照することです。少し保守的で、平凡すぎるようにも思いました。でも同時にヨーロッパの若い学生たちが持つ現代性と歴史性の両方の感覚を併せ持ったプロジェクトに感銘を受けることもあります。そういうときは歴史観の成熟を感じますね。

　日本人は現在直面している問題にいっせいに反応し、そしてすぐにそれを忘れてしまう傾向があるように思います。消費していると言うべきでしょうか。いまなにが面白いのか？　次に出てくるのは誰なのか？　建築はそれにどう答えるべきか？　もちろん、いま世の中でなにが起きているかを理解するのはとても大切です。でも一方で、建築はそう単純なものではないと思うのです。日本では建築の歴史感覚のスケールが短いことに起因しているのでしょう。

　でも2011年の東日本大震災以降、日本の社会は、そして日本の建築家のあいだでも、時間や歴史について再考しようという気運が高まってきています。これは大きな変化です。実際それは、私がヨーロッパの建築家たちに話を聞きに行ってみようと思ったひとつのきっかけでもあります。

1——ケイ・フィスカー(1893-1965)：デンマーク出身のモダニズム建築家。機能主義を唱える一方、その作風は北欧の煉瓦を活かした伝統的な意匠が特徴となっている。コペンハーゲンに多くの住宅を設計した。弟子にアルネ・ヤコブセンがいる。
2——アキ・カウリスマキ(1957-)：フィンランド出身の映画監督。代表作に『罪と罰』(1983)、『過去のない男』(2002)などがある。
3——パウロ・メンデス・ダ・ロシャ(1928-)：ブラジル出身の建築家。主な作品に《パウリスタノ・アスレチック・クラブ》(1957)や《サンペドロ教会》(1987)がある。2006年にプリツカー賞を受賞。
4——ヴィラノヴァ・アルティガス(1915-85)：ブラジル出身のモダニズム建築家。主な作品に《アルティガス自邸》(1949)、《サンパウロ大学都市建築学科棟》(1969)などがある。
5——サンパウロ派：1950年代、サンパウロを拠点として活動した建築家グループ。代表的な人物としてパウロ・メンデス・ダ・ロシャがいる。
6——カリオカ派：リオ・デ・ジャネイロを拠点とした建築家グループ。代表的な人物としてオスカー・ニーマイヤー(1907-2012)がいる。
7——ファヴェーラ・プロジェクト：ブラジルの大都市や郊外のスラム街を一般的にファヴェーラと呼ぶ。1960年代に撤去運動が起こったが失敗に終わり、その反省から2000年以降は、住民の生活の保障を目的としたファヴェーラ・プロジェクトが実施され、上下水道や道路舗装などのインフラ整備や労働支援の計画が進められた。
8——クリスチャン・ケレツ(1962-)：ヴェネズエラ出身、スイスで活動する建築家。主な作品に《オーバーレアルタの礼拝堂》(1992)、《ロイチェンバッハの学校》(2009)がある。
9——ヘルツォーク&ド・ムロン：ジャック・ヘルツォークとピエール・ド・ムロンの2人の建築家(いずれも1950-、スイス出身)により70年代末に設立された設計事務所。《シグナル・ボックス》(1994)、《プラダブティック青山》(2003)など、外皮のデザインに特化した作品を多く手がけている。

対話を終えて | After the conversation

パスカル・フラマーは今日注目されているスイスの若手建築家である。2014年からは母校であるスイス連邦工科大学チューリッヒ校で教鞭をとっている。対話は彼の処女作である《バルシュタールの住宅》で行なわれた。現在は彼の自宅兼オフィスとして使われている（もともとその計画ではなかったがクライアントがしばらく使わないことになり自分で住むことになったそうだ）。

フラマーの建築はスイスの建築家らしいコンセプチュアルな世界と、現実世界のあいだに鮮やかな協同関係をつくりあげる。2階建ての《バルシュタールの住宅》の下階は地面に750mm埋まり、上階は地面から僅か1500mmの高さに存在する。ともに地面からとても近く、空間と自然が特別な遭遇を見せている。例えば下階ではすぐ隣の大地に根を張るチューリップや家畜と自分が対等に存在していることに気づく。あるいはその向こう側に数km続く草原と地続きに存在していることにも。上階は地面を俯瞰するような高い位置にあるわけでもなく地続きでもなく、そのあいだ、まさに自分が宙づりにされているような感覚がある。彼の言う「人間の存在を問う」空間とはそういうことだろう。建築が強いアイデアや自律性をもちながらも、実際の経験としては現実世界を自分がどう受け止めているかという実感だけが残り、「建築が主張しない」ように配慮されている。

またフラマーは、20世紀前半のブラジルにおけるモダニズムの輸入、カニバリズムの思想を語った。「思想を自分たちが望むように、独自の解釈で調理」すること。それは単に歴史を参照することを超えて、自分たちのやり方で歴史を「料理する」という、より創造的で開かれたあり方を提示している。これまで建築家は「なにを食べるか」をしきりに議論し

Pascal Flammer is a young Swiss architect who is receiving a lot of attention these days. Since 2014 he has been teaching at his alma mater, ETH Zurich. We conducted the conversation at his first project, the House in Balsthal, which he currently uses as both residence and office. (That was not the original plan, he says, but when the client stopped using it he decided to live there himself.)

Flammer's architecture creates a brilliant collaborative relationship between the real world and a conceptual world typical of Swiss architects. The ground floor of the two-story House in Balsthal is buried 750 mm in the earth, and the upper floor extends only 1500 mm above ground level. Both floors are thus very close to the land, producing a unique encounter between living space and nature. For example, on the ground floor one feels that one exists on the same level as the tulips and farm animals in the field right next door... or as the expanse of meadowland that extends several kilometers beyond. The second floor is neither high enough to overlook the ground, nor is it one with the land, but somewhere in between, as if one were suspended in midair. This may be precisely what Flammer means by a space that is "a tool to question your own existence." Even when a building embodies strong ideas and autonomy, the physical experience of the building should leave you with only the sensation of how it makes you respond to the real world. Thus Flammer's concern is that a building "should not indicate anything."

Flammer also touches on Brazil's assimilation of modernist concepts in the early 20th century, a process he calls "cannibalism": "They

てきたのかもしれない。それに対して「どうやって自分たちのやり方で調理してどこまで食べ尽くせるか」というカニバリズムの思想には、ある種の危険さを感じるとともに、惹かれるものがある。グローバル化が進んだ現代、世界中の大量の情報が次々になだれ込んできて、表層的なデザインの消費は容易に行なわれるようになったが、出会ったことのない新たな思想に感化され、それを自らの環境で育み、再解釈していく経験は20世紀よりもむしろ少なくなっているように思う。そうした閉塞感に対して、僕は例えばこの本で対抗しようとしているのかもしれない。現代建築における開かれたカニバリズムはいかに可能だろうか。

ate them to their own taste, in the way they wanted." What he means is that the Brazilians did not merely reference history, but, in a more creative and liberating fashion, "cooked" history according to their own recipe. Until now, perhaps architects have been arguing among themselves about "what to eat." The cannibalistic viewpoint — "How shall we prepare the meal, and how much shall we eat?" — is both potentially dangerous and seductive. In the current age of globalization, we are exposed to a constant avalanche of information from all over, facilitating the ready consumption of superficial designs. But it seems to me that we are less likely now than in the 20th century to experience inspiration from a new way of thinking we have never encountered before, then nurture and reinterpret it in our own environment. Perhaps it is in reaction to this feeling of isolation that I put together this book. Is a more liberating cannibalism possible in the world of contemporary architecture?

Pascal Flammer

2つの階段のあるオフィス／2000
Office with Two Stairs/2000

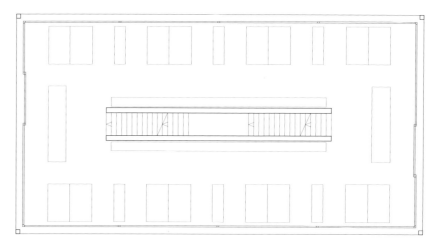

2階平面図　1:200
second floor plan 1:200

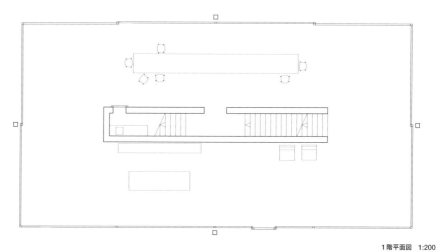

1階平面図　1:200
first floor plan 1:200

Pascal Flammer

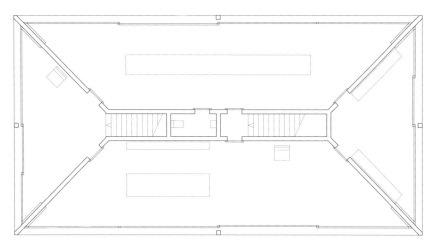

3階平面図 1:200
third floor plan 1:200

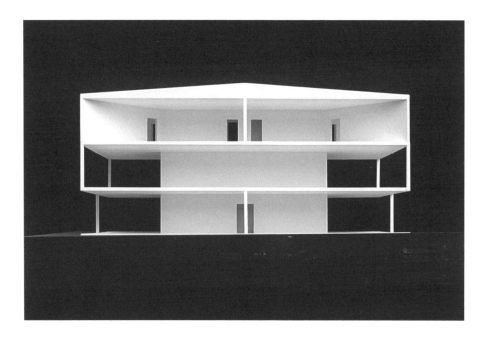

Pascal Flammer

Office with Two Stairs

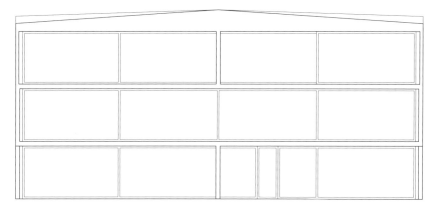

立面図 1:200
elevation 1:200

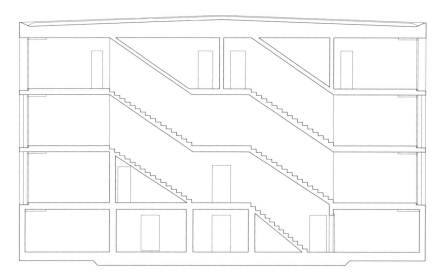

断面図図 1:200
section 1:200

Pascal Flammer

バルシュタールの住宅／スイス／2012
House in Balsthal/Switzerland/2012

Pascal Frammer

バルシュタールの住宅
House in Balsthal

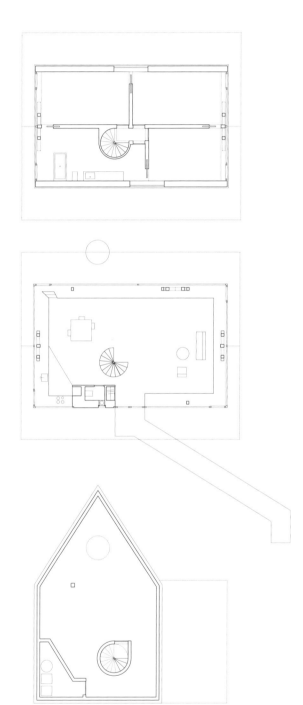

地階、1 階、2 階平面図　1:250
basement, first, and second floor plan 1:250

Pascal Flammer

Pascal Flammer

バルシュタールの住宅
House in Balsthal

Pascal Flammer

Pascal Flammer

House in Balsthal

Pascal Flammer

Pascal Flammer

フリオ・オトニのコミュニティ・センター／2005
Centro Comunitário Júlio Otoni / 2005

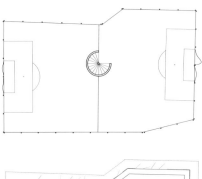

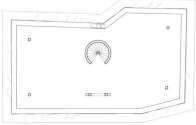

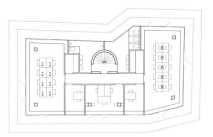

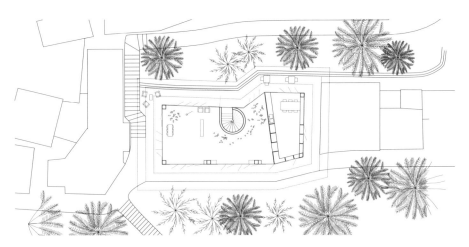

1階、2階、3階、屋上平面図
first, second, third floor, and roof plan

Pascal Flammer

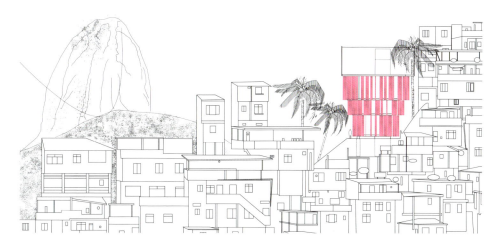

立面図
elevation

Kersten Geers & David Van Severen

24th May 2014
@ OFFICE Kersten Geers David Van Severen, Brussels, Belgium

Kersten Geers & David Van Severen

OFFICE for engineers

Go Hasegawa How did you arrive at your firm's name, "OFFICE"? You also name your works "OFFICE 39" and such—what's that all about?

David Van Severen We liked how Belgian fashion designers use just their names—Ann Demeulemeester, Dries Van Noten, and so on. It's an authorship. But in our case we needed something to combine our two names. Putting "office" in front did the trick.

Kersten Geers And we're talking 2003, so it was still at the tail end of the Dutch architecture movement, when every office did its best to have the weirdest name. We say it two ways—either it's OFFICE Kersten Geers David van Severen, or it's OFFICE, period. It's one or the other, so either we disappear behind the moniker, or we take on all responsibility.

To me, an office is an extremely horizontal place. Of course we have a clear hierarchy in decision-making—in the end the two of us sitting here at this table are responsible—but I think it has grown in such a way that the people who work for us are very much there and involved, very much a part of it. So the horizontal or democratic notion of office is, when you look at us today, very much a part of who we are.

DVS Maybe there's also a slight fascination for neutrality. Today everyone is an "atelier" or a "studio." By contrast, "office" has some kind of boring neutrality to it. A dryness.

KG   David tends to say that we are engineers. We are not architects in the sense of artists. We are not artistic. Of course we hold that we have good taste, but we think of ourselves foremost as engineers—thus "office" rather than "atelier." We're not the type to take up pencils and start to draw, that's not our approach. We come from a polytechnic school, where you study engineering and architecture, and in some strange way we are proud of that. Our projects are technically sound, meaning we know what we do.

DVS   I like the idea that building draws also on knowledge from different engineering fields. It can be almost mathematical, too. We like this kind of dryness. But all of this was completely unconscious, you know. We probably sound like we're very aware of these things, but we weren't back when we started!

What is classic?

GH   Your works do carry a solid image of engineering and math, but at the same time I feel a sort of European sense—something classic, a mix of old and new. I'm curious, what's your take on history?

KG   History is fundamental to us. But classic is not necessarily a style. I think that classic is in many ways fundamental. It's not like classic is all about columns and rhythm, right? It's rather about being able to develop a body of work completely disconnected from how people judge it. In order to be a cultural producer, you can only be classic. To that extent I would argue that Ed Ruscha[1] is classic, too. It's about developing a body of work that is entirely busy with its own consistency. It understands that it's part of the context of cultural production, and it accepts the logic of the market. Now, the market is such that maybe you're successful, maybe you're not. And if you are successful it might be for the wrong reason, but you are successful nevertheless. If I look at the few architects whose work we really admire—like Álvaro Siza—this notion of classic is fundamentally there. If I look at artists—Ruscha, for example—something classic is there. They have a discourse, and that discourse is not simplifiable. Through their new works we find another piece of a universe that we begin to understand. Most of these people wouldn't be able to explain to you why they did what they did, only that they somehow felt it was right. And I think that is the core of what makes something classic. In many ways, that's what we're after. I sense that the people whose work I deeply appreciate were seeking it, too. What else can you say, I think the pursuit of the classic is the only way.

GH   Which works from your portfolio would you say fit that definition best?

DVS   In a way what is very typical about the classical is that it makes an abstraction of what we know as natural. Classic is not a style but an attitude. It is like this in our work. Our Colonnade project [fig.1] now under development in Jette shows this. What is striking about classic is that it is not concerned about program, but rather space. Colonnade presents one major asset, the court, around which the program functions. The housing, in a way, is not important in this project. Sure, it activates the court and gives it life, but the purpose really is the colonnaded courtyard, which, in being pulled through to the street, makes a gesture that is both public and cultural.

KG   I would add that nobody desperately wants to emulate something from the past. Yet on the other hand, we operate in full knowledge of the past. Because that's our context. If you walk out of that context, you're in an open sea. You have nothing to gain, nothing to lose. In many ways, I still hope, deep inside, that a figure like Rem Koolhaas[2] is doing that too. But that's the game he plays. As an author, being so intelligent, he deeply understands that line, and he walks it. Unlike most other authors of that intelligence, he often walks that line to fall. But that's not a bad thing.

Koolhaas and Belgium

GH   We all started to study in the late 1990s, a time when architecture in Switzerland and Holland was very hot also for Japanese students. Herzog & de Meuron, and Koolhaas, of course.

I see your work as a kind of post-Koolhaas architecture. Of course you are Belgian, but you worked in Holland, and you came after Koolhaas.

KG   It would be naive to pretend that we're free from Dutch influences. Those times influenced us as students. But at the same time, we were not happy with how architecture was conceived in Holland in the late 1990s and early into the next decade. So in that sense I think we are post-Koolhaas. I remember very well in 1995, when I was a second-year student and that gigantic book *S, M, L, XL* was released and became an instant megahit. Koolhaas was mainstream after that. At the same time, he was the only one who defined a new culture of architecture. When I finished university, there were people in Belgium like Stéphane Beel[3] and Xaveer De Geyter[4], and in Holland there was OMA itself, and also MVRDV[5]. So it was clear that in Belgium, there were plenty of people who were under the influence of OMA.

The years from 1999 to 2001 were a pivotal time in Europe. Holland was doing well but at the same time there were other things on the rise. And we had been studying with Ábalos & Herreros[6] in Madrid.

DVS   I think we should not underestimate Ábalos & Herreros in this story, in the sense that they were dry but they also had a lot of knowledge about and opinions of their own context as well as the history of architecture. And they selected very precise episodes.

I think they are architects' architects. They made a couple of very beautiful buildings, but their beauty is not in the details. Their work is kind of blunt, harsh, and direct. I don't think it's easy to like. They would make boxes out of metal pieces and panel systems and sunscreens. There was seemingly no complexity in their work. There was a box, there was nothing spectacular, no constructive innovation. They showed us the beauty of the banal.

GH I see. And how did you view Koolhaas after finishing your studies?

KG Architecture became, or remained, a cultural profession. That's a bit of a strange statement, because we tend to claim a certain skepticism toward OMA. But at the same time I think there was no architect that was more important, also to us, than Koolhaas. I mean, he was fundamental. We were looking at his work from a non-Dutch angle.

I think we both agree that Koolhaas is the least Dutch of all Dutch architects. He always has an ambiguity—what you see is not what you get, it's confusing. In Holland, architects became successful over the last 100 years through Dutch modernism and everything that came after that—structuralism and so forth—and started to play a social role. They were very much embedded in society. There was no cultural narrative. The architect was a trusted partner in building the society we would share. In Belgium, there were never such big opportunities.

DVS He also used a certain idiosyncrasy from Belgium. The entire Villa Dall'Ava (1991) is built by Belgian construction, and some details were designed by a Belgian—my father.

GH Really?

DVS Yeah, it's true, because there was no craftsmanship of that level in France at that time—nor today, either. Koolhaas knew how to find that talent.

KG I think there are many architects today in Belgium who are much more inspired by the British model, which is funny, because the British model actually came through Robbrecht & Daem[7], who became a cornerstone for a whole concept of architecture that was furthered in England by Caruso St. John[8], Sergison Bates[9], and so on. In the end it's more or less us who have been deeply influenced by this metropolitan view of architecture. It's a very complex view, because it's European architecture translated by east-coast American theories brought back to Europe. We dissect it and represent it through architecture again. So it's a very strange, mutated version of architecture.

It's funny, when I was teaching at the Academy of Architecture in Mendrisio I felt that it was not really Switzerland. It felt like something else. And while we really admire the works of Lacaton & Vassal, we are not French architects, we're something else. As David points out, ours is a strange combination of craftsmanship with a metropolitan view and discourse—not in the Swiss way, not super expensive. This combination never happened in Holland because they don't embrace craftsmanship. It doesn't happen in Switzerland because they don't understand the city. And it doesn't happen in France because they have no relationship with craftsmanship.

GH   I see. Craftsmanship and metropolitan view.

KG   France was crucial to Koolhaas. He was making projects for Lille (1989-1994), he was doing the Très Grande Bibliothèque (1989), he was doing the two Jussieu Libraries (1992)—at least trying; he was doing the Villa Dall'Ava (1991) and Villa in Bordeaux (1998), especially from the 1990s, that's what he did. And we were literally in the middle of Holland and France. He is a Belgian architect in the sense that he's from Holland, but working in France, meanwhile crossing Belgium and taking all its good craftsmen, taking the designers, taking the architects. Take any of his projects in France—they're Belgian projects. So if you ask why is Belgium currently important, I would say because Koolhaas was a Belgian architect.

GH   I never expected to hear that. But it's interesting, and might underscore the potential here in Belgium today, geographically set in the center of Western Europe.

DVS   Exactly!

Measuring system and space for life

GH   Today I was able to visit four of your buildings. I found a kind of simple grid system in each one—the four square rooms of the OFFICE 56 Weekend House in Merchtem (2012) [fig.2], nine square rooms of the OFFICE 39 Villa in Buggenhout (2010) [fig.3], the colonnade of the OFFICE 62 City Villa in Brussels (2012), and the PC panel wall of the OFFICE 90 Agriculture School in Leuven (2014) [fig.4, 5]. I found it interesting that several times you have mentioned measuring. Tell me about this measuring system. What do you measure? What's your aim?

KG   I would almost dare to say that the most important thing you can do as an architect is introduce a set of references, a ruler, a measuring system. It's almost like a trace of culture. So there is something there, and you don't necessarily want to change that, but you do want to be able to grasp it, to control it to a certain extent. This idea of measuring, like a Cartesian grid, is very important for that.

There's a word painting by Ed Ruscha called "Talk about Space." The tiny pencil in it is painted in full size, one to one. It allows you to measure the work, the tableau. It also allows you to measure, in some strange way, space. "Talk about Space," you could say, is also measuring space.

So this idea that you introduce elements to use as reference to something you cannot completely control is in many ways a common thread that runs through all our work. Call it classicism, rationalism, or other things, it always goes back to this attempt to make something part of a system, but at the same time allowing exceptions to that system. And exceptions are, of course, only possible as soon as you have put in enough effort to establish the system. If there is only exception, there is no system. So I think there is a search for equilibrium in our projects — more system than exception. This happens in many different ways and scales, and sometimes very literally.

DVS Measuring is repetition. A unit needs a second to make it a system. In the four rooms of the Weekend House, the nine (or actually 18 because it has two floors) rooms of Buggenhout, and the City Villa where columns frame the rooms, the common factor is rhythm [fig.6]. Rhythm frames the rooms. Creating rhythms or a multiplication of things is important, as it begins a background and foreground conversation where you see and yet don't see, and it is the architecture that gives you the power to understand that discourse.

GH I also notice in your buildings a sort of materiality that exists in parallel with their strong forms. Your system controls the space very clearly, but it looks very natural. You achieve an equilibrium between architecture and nature that I can relate to.

KG I must say that when I saw your buildings in Tokyo — I went to the wooden house (House in Komazawa, 2011) [fig.7] and the steel-roof house (House in Kyodo, 2011) — it was amazing. I saw a lot of parallels. I got the impression that the negotiations behind each decision on the materials — let's say, for the wooden house, how you make the floor, what you close, what you don't close, the shelf, the stair, and so on — I thought that was all very similar to how we make decisions. And the wooden house carried something more than an organizational idea. Through its material, it became a special place. The same can be said of the steel house. Our buildings are bigger, but they are very similar. And there are not so many architects who do things like that.

I've visited the Müller House (1928-30) by Adolf Loos[10], and it's so beautiful. It's also far more radical than I thought it was from the pictures, because he presents things in strange relationships, too. On the one hand the house, on the outside, is white, with these yellow windows, but when you're inside it has this crazy marble and very nice wood. All these elements lure you into a certain way of use. It's not exactly decoration.

I like materials that seem to represent something else. You could say it's similar to Aldo Rossi's[11] concept of memory. Not memory of the city, but simply the idea that pure, abstract architecture does not exist. Whatever you build, there will be a certain memory of another building, another space in that construction. And that is fascinating.

GH In the Buggenhout Villa I sensed an architecture that places great value on the joy of life. This belief in life seems to me to be a very strong statement of your architectural discourse.

KG In terms of life, quite frankly I have learned a lot from David. Before we met, I didn't have this direct experience of life as extreme or hedonistic, because I came from another background. David always had this enormous laissez-faire sense about things. There was at least this celebration of life, all the time. His father was extremely hedonistic. David grew up like that. And I think that this, plus our LA experiences and fascinations when we were students, is what made us make things that were never constructions or ideas about architecture. They were really very close to life. I think it came from that place.

Life is full of ambiguities, so let's allow them to happen. It's how it is. You can't change that. From that perspective, it should come rather easily!

OFFICE without OFFICE

GH My last question is about architectural education. You are teaching now at Swiss Federal Institute of Technology Lausanne (EPF Lausanne). Do you like to teach? And do you see any relation between teaching in the university and your practice at the office?

KG I have to teach in order to think. That's the only reason I teach. I need to discuss. I know some people who only teach about their own architecture. That's not how I approach it. When I teach, I talk about other things, but of course, talking about other things is a trick to find out about what it is you want to say. That's the key of teaching for me. And I like it.

It's important that you meet, from time to time, somebody who motivates you. So, when you meet the better student—and sometimes you do—I think it's important not to make them too comfortable. Unfortunately, there are not so many of these now. There are a lot of average students.

In teaching, you sometimes have this situation where some students do not really progress. It can be frustrating, but if the discussion has been about things that matter, that's good. Trying to get through to them makes you question what it is that you consider important. I don't think that what we propose as architecture is "the" architecture. At the same time, I would like to keep on questioning myself, and I think teaching is a very good way to do that—because you actually do that, as well as the inverse—but the act of teaching does not in the end need to influence what you do yourself. It might influence it a bit, like an echo, but not completely. And I think that's a luxury. The act of teaching allows you to think, but without direct impact, somehow. That's why, recently, I started to make these little booklets in the studio, "OFFICE without OFFICE." For me that would be the perfect place. It's where you do your work, but you remove any commercial logic. My main argument was that I believe it's still possible to operate disconnected from a market. Whether you want it or not, you can be the most radical architect and there is still a commercial logic to that, even. So, for me, you could say there is this office, and to a certain extent, as I've started to see it in my head, my teaching is like "OFFICE without OFFICE."

GH "OFFICE without OFFICE." We began this conversation with "OFFICE," so we've come full circle!

1 —— Ed Ruscha: American contemporary artist born in 1937. Major works include "IF" (2000)" and "Pay Nothing Until April" (2003), characterized by a conceptual style using texts.
2 —— Rem Koolhaas: Dutch architect born in 1944. Since establishing Office for Metropolitan Architecture in mid-1970's, he has undertaken widespread activities ranging from urban research to publication. Other than major built works including Maison à Bordeaux (1998) and Seattle Public Library (2004), he is also known for authoring *Delirious New York* (1978) and *S, M, L, XL* (1995).
3 —— Stéphane Beel: Belgian architect born in 1955. Major works include House M (1992), and together with Xaveer De Geyter, Faculty of Economics Ghent University (2006).
4 —— Xaveer De Geyter: Belgian architect born in 1957. Founder of XDGA. Former member of OMA in the 1980s. Major projects include Ilot Saint Maurice Urban Plan (1996-) and Chasse Park Apartments (2003).
5 —— MVRDV: Dutch architectural office established in early 1990's. Founders Winy Maas (born 1959) and Jacob van Rijs (born 1964) once worked for OMA. Major projects include Netherlands Pavilion at the 2000 World Expo in Hanover (2000).
6 —— Ábalos & Herreros: Architecture office founded by two Spanish architects. Iñaki Ábalos was born in 1956, and Juan Herreros was born in 1958. Major works include Usera Public Library (2002). The office dissolved in 2008.
7 —— Robbrecht & Daem: Architecture office founded by two Belgian architects, Paul Robbrecht and Hilde Daem, both born in 1950. Major works include Concert Hall Bruges (2002) and Market Hall (2013).
8 —— Caruso St. John: Architecture office founded by two British architects, Adam Caruso and Peter St. John, born in 1962 and 1959 respectively. Major commissions include Tate Britain, Millbank Project (2013).
9 —— Sergison Bates: Architecture office founded by two British architects, Jonathan Sergison and Stephen Bates, both born in 1963. Major works include Mixed Use Development in Wandsworth (2004) and Centre for Applied Arts in Ruthin (2008).
10 —— Adolf Loos: Austrian architect born in 1870 and deceased in 1933. Best known for developing architectural exteriors without ornamentations and the "Raumplan," a unique method in which spaces are configured three-dimensionally. Representative works include Villa Müller (1930), and the book *Ornament and Crime* (1908).
11 —— Aldo Rossi: Italian architect born in 1931 and deceased in 1997. Known principally for Gallaratese Housing Complex (1973), Teatro del Mondo (1979), and for authoring *The Architecture of the City* (1966) and *A Scientific Autobiography* (1981).

Kersten Geers & David Van Severen

ケルステン・ゲールス &
ダヴィッド・ファン・セーヴェレン

2014年5月24日
ベルギー、ブリュッセル、オフィス・ケルステン・ゲールス・
ダヴィッド・ファン・セーヴェレンにて

エンジニアたちのオフィス

長谷川 豪(以下、GH) あなたたちは自分たちの事務所名を「OFFICE(オフィス)」とし、作品を《OFFICE 39》のように呼んでいますよね。これにはどういった思惑があるのでしょうか?

ダヴィッド・ファン・セーヴェレン(以下、DVS) アン・ドゥムルメステールやドリス・ヴァン・ノッテンといったベルギーのファッションデザイナーたちが、ブランド名としてシンプルに自分の名前だけを使うのが私は好きなんです。作家名で活動している人たちです。私たちの場合は、2人組なのでお互いの名前をつなげる言葉が必要でした。頭に「OFFICE」をつけることでその問題を解決しました。

ケルステン・ゲールス(以下、KG) 独立して事務所名を議論していたのは2003年頃のことでした。ちょうどオランダ建築の盛り上がりのまっただなかで、当時は皆、奇妙な事務所名を競って考えていましたね。私たちが自分たちの事務所を呼ぶときには、2つの呼称を使っています。オフィス・ケルステン・ゲールス・ダヴィッド・ファン・セーヴェレン、あるいは単にオフィス.(ピリオド)です。「オフィス」という略称を隠れ蓑にすることもあれば、名前を前面に出すことで責任の所在を明確にすることもあります。

　オフィスというのはヒエラルキーのないフラットな場所だと思います。もちろん、意思決定においては明確なヒエラルキーが存在し、最終的には、いまこのテーブルに座っている私たち2人が責任を負うことになります。でもここで仕事をする

人たちは皆、主体的で責任感もあり、意思決定のなかでも大きな役割を果たしています。私たちのオフィスはそういう組織なのです。ですから今日見てもらってわかったかと思いますが、水平的で民主的な私たちのオフィスの性格は、私たち自身の反映でもあります。

DVS おそらく私たちはニュートラルであるということに魅力を感じているのだと思います。いまは、どこもかしこも「アトリエ」あるいは「スタジオ」であろうとします。これに対して、「オフィス」はある意味で凡庸でニュートラルな性格を持っています。ドライなんですね。

KG ダヴィッドはよく、私たちはエンジニアであると言います。私たちは芸術家を連想させるような建築家ではありません。芸術家肌ではないのです。もちろん私たちはいいセンスを持っていると思います。でもむしろエンジニアでありたいと思っています。「アトリエ」ではなく「オフィス」と名乗るのもそのためです。鉛筆を取り出しておもむろに描きはじめるのは私たちのやり方ではないのです。工学系の大学で建築学と工学を学びましたが、私たちはその出自を誇りに思っています。私たちはプロジェクトを技術的に裏づけながら進めています。

DVS 建物がほかの工学分野の知を応用するという考え方も気に入っています。数学的と言ってもいいかもしれませんが、客観性を好んでいます。でも基本的には客観的であるかどうかはあまり意識しないようにしています。私たちがはじめから意識しているように思われるかもしれませんが、プロジェクトがある程度進んだ段階ではじめて意識化されるのだと思います。

古典の定義とはなにか

GH たしかにあなたたちの作品は工学や数学に通じるものを感じさせます。しかしそれと同時に、私はヨーロッパ的なものも感じます。古典的というか、伝統的なものと新しいものが共存しているような。あなたたちが歴史をどのように捉えているか訊かせてもらえますか。

KG 歴史は私たちにとって根源的なものです。でも古典的であるということはかならずしも様式を示してはいないのです。古典的であることもまたいろいろな意味で根源的なものです。べつに柱やリズムだけが古典を意味するわけではないですよ

ね。そうではなくむしろ他人の評価とは別次元で自分の作品を体系づけられるかどうかということかもしれません。文化を牽引する者であるためには古典的でなくてはなりません。その意味でエド・ルシェ[1]は古典的です。彼は自分の価値観を貫いた作品体系の構築に執心しています。それは文化の創造というコンテクストで理解されるべきものですが、その一方でマーケットの論理も受け入れています。

　マーケットは気まぐれですから、成功するかどうかは予測できません。もし成功したとしてもあまりよくない理由からかもしれません。それでも成功は成功です。私たちが尊敬する何人かの建築家、例えばアルヴァロ・シザのような建築家の作品の根底には、古典的であることに通じるものが存在します。アーティストはといえば、例えばルシェにもなにか古典に通じるものが存在します。なにかを主張していますが、それは単純化できるものではありません。新しい作品を通じて、彼らが持つ世界観の新しい側面を発見できます。これらの作家たちは、自分の創作を論理的に説明することはしませんが、感覚的に正しいと信じてやっているわけです。それがまさに古典的であるということなのだと思います。私たちはそれを目指しています。私が敬愛する作家たちもそれを求めているような気がします。古典的であり続けることは唯一の道のように思えます。

GH　あなたたちのこれまでの作品のなかで、いま話されたことに最もよく当てはまるものはどれでしょうか？

DVS　古典的であるかどうかということは、すでに明らかだと思っているものを抽象化できているかどうかだと思います。古典的であることは、様式ではなく態度にかかわることです。少なくとも私たちの作品においてはそうです。私たちがブリュッセルのジェット地区で取り組んでいるコロネード（列柱）のプロジェクト [fig.1] はそれをよく表現していると思います。古典的なものは、プログラムよりも空間を重視しているため強度を持ちます。コロネード・プロジェクトでは、大きな中庭のまわりにさまざまなプログラムが配置されていますが、住宅という機能はもしかしたらこのプロジェクトにとってさほど重要ではないかもしれません。もちろん、住宅であることが中庭を意味のある、そして生き生きとしたものにします。でもこのプロジェクトで重要なのは、柱が並ぶ中庭であり、それがストリートまで延伸されることで公共的で文化的な場所になることです。

KG　ひとつ付け加えるとすると、昔のものを必死になって真似ようとする人はいません。その一方で、私たちの創作は過去の知の上に成り立っています。それが私

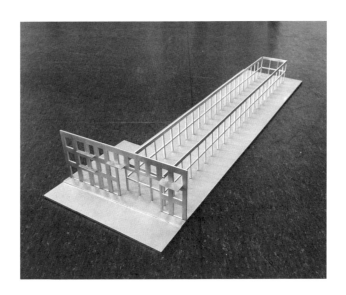

fig.1　OFFICE 155 コロネード・プロジェクト
OFFICE 155 Colonnade Project

たちのコンテクストだからです。もしそのコンテクストから距離をとってしまうと未知の海に放り出されることになります。なにも得るものはなく、失うものもありません。レム・コールハース[2]のような建築家もいろいろな意味でいまもコンテクストを重視していると私は信じています。でも彼はそれをゲームとしてやっています。とても頭が切れる作家ですから、彼はそのコンテクストを理解してその上を歩いていますが、ほかの作家と違ってあえて踏み外しながら歩いています。それもそれでひとつのやり方です。

コールハースとベルギー

GH　私もちょうど90年代後半に建築を学びはじめましたが、当時は日本の建築学生にとってもスイスとオランダの建築がとても勢いのあった時期でした。その代表がヘルツォーク＆ド・ムロンとコールハースです。
　あなたたちの作品は、コールハース以降の建築だと言えると思います。もちろんあなたたちがベルギー人だということはわかっていますが、オランダで仕事をしていたこともあるし、コールハース以降の世代ですよね。

KG　オランダ建築の影響を受けていないふりをするのはナイーヴかもしれませんね。当時学生だった私たちは、その時代から大きな影響を受けました。でも一方で私たちは90年代後半から2000年代前半にかけてのオランダでの建築の受容のされ

方に違和感も感じていました。その意味で私たちはコールハース以降の建築家と言えるかもしれません。1995年は私たちは大学2年生でしたが、『S, M, L, XL』という例の分厚い本が出版され、瞬く間にバカ売れしたのを覚えています。コールハースはその直後から建築界のメインストリームになりました。当時、彼は建築に新しいカルチャーを持ち込んだ唯一の人物でした。私が卒業した頃、ベルギーにはステファン・ベール[3]、ザヴェール・デ・ヘイテル[4]といった建築家がいましたが、オランダにはOMAがいましたし、MVRDV[5]もいました。ベルギーにもOMAの影響を受けた建築家がたくさんいたのは確かですね。

　1999年から2001年はヨーロッパにとってひとつの転換点です。オランダは活況を呈していましたが、別の動きが胎動していました。私たちがマドリードでアバロス&ヘレロス[6]の下で勉強していたときです。

DVS　この話の流れでアバロス&ヘレロスをきちんと取り上げるべきですね。彼らはあっさりしているように見えるかもしれませんが、知識も豊富ですし、彼ら自身のコンテクストについての考えだけでなく、建築の歴史についてもしっかりとした立ち位置を持っているんです。エピソードの選び方も秀逸です。

　彼らは建築家のなかの建築家だと思います。とても美しい建物を設計しますが、彼らの建築の美しさはディテールだけに宿るわけではありません。彼らの作品はぶっきらぼうで、荒々しく、ひねりもありません。好き嫌いが分かれるかもしれませんね。メタルやパネル、日よけスクリーンなどを纏った箱型の建物が多く、複雑さに欠けているようにも見えます。ただの箱。スペクタクルもなく、構造的な挑戦もない。彼らからは単純であることの美学を学びました。

GH　なるほど。マドリードで勉強した後、コールハースに対する見方は変わりましたか？

KG　建築が文化の創造にかかわる職能だと思うようになりました。OMAに対するある種の疑念を持ちはじめていたはずなのでちょっと不思議な気もしますね。でも、私たちにとってもやはりコールハースほど重要な建築家はいません。彼は踏まえるべき基礎になったのです。私たちは彼をオランダ建築とは違うものとして見られるようになったのでしょう。

　コールハースは、オランダの建築家のなかでも最もオランダ的でないと思います。つねに両義性をもっていて、見え方と中身が違うので混乱してしまうんですよね。オランダでは、オランダ近代建築やその後の構造主義建築などが続いたこの

100年のあいだに建築家がとても成功し、社会的な役割を担うようになりました。つまり社会と密接にかかわる職能になったので、文化的な職能ではなくなったということです。建築家は社会を構築する職能として市民に信頼されるようになったのです。ベルギーはまだそこまでいっていません。

DVS　一方でコールハースはベルギーの優位性も利用しています。《ダラヴァ邸》(1991) はベルギーの技術で施工されており、いくつかのディテールはベルギー人がデザインしたんですよ。実は私の父なんですが。

GH　本当ですか？

DVS　本当です。当時、フランスにはそれほどの高い施工技術はなかったし、いまもありません。コールハースは必要な才能をどこで調達すべきかわかっていたのです。

KG　いま、ベルギーにはイギリスからの影響を受けた建築家が多くいます。もともとはロブレヒト・エン・ダーム[7]が提唱した概念をイギリスで継承したカルーゾ・セント・ジョン[8]やサージソン・ベイツ[9]といった建築家によって、イギリス的なコンセプトがもたらされたので、ちょっとややこしいですね。そのような都市的な建築に影響を受けて登場したのがおそらく私たちかもしれません。ヨーロッパの建築は、アメリカ東海岸での言説を経由してヨーロッパに逆輸入されているため、とても錯綜しています。私たちはそれを咀嚼し、建築を通じて表現しているので、かなり奇妙なことになっています。突然変異的な建築といえるでしょう。

　でもメンドリシオ建築アカデミーで教えていたとき、不思議なことにそこがスイスではないと感じました。まったく別な場所に思えたのです。例えばラカトン＆ヴァッサルの作品が好きだというとき、私たちはフランス人建築家としてではなく、まったく別な存在として評価しています。ダヴィッドが指摘したように、私たちの建築は、職人的なものと都市的な視点や言説が共存した不思議なものです。スイス的でもなく、お金のかかる建築でもありません。このような共存はオランダではありえないでしょうね。彼らは職人的なことを重視しません。スイスでもありえないでしょう。彼らは都市的なことを理解しません。フランスでもありえません。職人的なものと無関係だからです。

GH　なるほど。職人的であることと都市的であることの共存がベルギーの特徴だと。

KG　フランスはコールハースを冷遇しています。《リール都市開発プロジェクト》（1989-94）をやったし、「フランス国立国会図書館」（1989）、「ジュシュー図書館」（1992）といったコンペ案があり、《ダラヴァ邸》（1991）も《ボルドーの住宅》（1998）もあります。彼は90年代以降にフランスでこれだけのことをやったんですよ。ベルギーは地理的にはオランダとフランスのあいだに位置しています。コールハースはオランダ出身で、フランスでプロジェクトをしたという意味でベルギー的な建築家と言えます。フランスへの道中、ベルギーを通過していくときに優れた職人、デザイナー、そして建築家を発掘し引き連れていったのです。彼のフランスのプロジェクトは、どれもベルギー人による仕事です。なぜいまベルギーの建築が重要なのかといえば、それはコールハースがベルギー的な建築家だからです。

GH　それははじめて聞きました。面白いですね。地理的に西ヨーロッパの中心に位置しているという、今日のベルギーの可能性を裏付ける話ですね。

DVS　その通り！

定量化の方法と生きるための空間

GH　今日、あなたたちが設計した4つの建物を見せていただきました。《OFFICE 56 メルシュテムのウィークエンド・ハウス》（2012）[fig.2]の4つの正方形から成るプラン、《OFFICE 39 バーゲンホフトのヴィラ》（2010）の3×3の9部屋のプラン[fig.3]、《OFFICE 62 ブリュッセルのシティ・ヴィラ》（2012）のコロネード、そして《OFFICE 90 ルーヴェンの農学校》（2014）[fig.4, 5]のPCパネルの外壁など、どれにも共通するものとしてシンプルなグリッドシステムがあります。あなたたちはよく定量化（measuring）について話をしていますが、定量化の仕組みについて少し説明してもらえますか？　なにを定量化し、なぜ定量化するのでしょうか。

KG　建築家ができることで最も重要なことはレファレンス、ガイドライン、定量化システムを示すことだと考えています。つまり、ある場所にすでになにかが存在していたとして、特になにかを変える必要はないけれど、そのなにかを把握し、コントロールすることが重要なのです。この定量化という方法は、デカルト・グリッドのように、とても重要なものです。
　《空間について語る》（1963）という題のエド・ルシェの絵画があります。絵画のな

fig.2 OFFICE 56 メルシュテムのウィークエンド・ハウス
OFFICE 56 Weekend House in Merchtem

配置図 1:800
site plan 1:800

Kersten Geers & David Van Severen

Kersten Geers & David Van Severen

fig.3 OFFICE 39 バーゲンホフトのヴィラ (2010)
OFFICE 39 Villa in Buggenhout, 2010

fig.4, 5　OFFICE 90 ルーヴェンの農業学校（2014）
OFFICE 90 Agriculture School in Leuven, 2014

Kersten Geers & David Van Severen

かに原寸大の小さな鉛筆が描かれていますが、それで絵画の大きさを測ることができますし、まるで空間そのものを測ることもできそうです。《空間について語る》というあの作品も、空間を定量化しているんです。

　レファレンスとなるようななにか、それも完全にはコントロールできないようななにかを組み込むというアイデアは私たちの作品に一貫して見られるものだと思います。古典主義にせよ、合理主義にせよ、あるいはほかのなにかにせよ、すべての要素をシステムに組み込もうとしますが、同時にシステムからの例外も許容しています。もちろん、例外が許容されることは確固たるシステムが構築されてはじめて可能になります。例外のみが存在すればそもそもシステムは成立しません。私たちのプロジェクトでは例外を許容しうるシステムという平衡状態のようなものを模索しています。いろいろな方法やスケールでやりますし、ときには直截的にやることもあります。

DVS　定量化することは反復するということでもあります。ひとつのユニットは次のユニットがあってはじめてシステムになります。《OFFICE 56 メルシュテムのウィークエンド・ハウス》の4つの部屋、《OFFICE 39 バーゲンホフトのヴィラ》の9つの部屋——実際には2階建てなので18の部屋ですが——そして柱が部屋をフレーミングしている《OFFICE 62 ブリュッセルのシティ・ヴィラ》[fig.6]において共通する要素はリズムです。リズムが部屋を規定します。私たちはリズムを生み出したり、モノを複数化することを重視しています。それは見えるものと見えないもの、図と地の対話の始まりであり、その関係性を理解するきっかけを与えてくれます。

GH　なるほど。次に素材について訊かせてください。あなたたちの作品には強い形式とマテリアリティが同時に感じられます。空間が明確に規定されていますが、それはとても自然なものに感じられます。建築的であることと、自然であることが無理なく共存して実現されている、それは私が共感するところでもあります。

KG　東京であなたの建築——木造の住宅(《駒沢の住宅》2011) [fig.7]とスチール屋根の住宅(《経堂の住宅》2011)——を見ましたが、素晴らしかった。私たちとあなたの共通点をたくさん発見できました。素材に関する意思決定の背後にある考え方——例えば、木造の住宅での床の考え方、どこを閉じて、どこを開けるのか、棚や階段などのあり方——から、私たちの意思決定との共通点を感じました。木造の住宅は、建物全体の構成以上の思想があるように感じられました。素材の使い方によって特別な場所になっています。スチール屋根の住宅についても同じことです。

fig.6　OFFICE 62　ブリュッセルのシティ・ヴィラ（2012）
OFFICE 62 City Villa in Brussels, 2012

Kersten Geers & David Van Severen

Kersten Geers & David Van Severen

fig.7 長谷川豪《駒沢の住宅》(2011)
Go Hasegawa, House in Komazawa, 2011

　私たちの建物はあなたの建物に比べて規模が大きいですが、でも両者はとても似ています。このようなことをする建築家はさほど多くはないでしょう。

　アドルフ・ロース[10]の《ミュラー邸》(1930)を訪ねたことがあるのですが、それはとても美しかったです。そして写真で見るよりもラディカルでした。意外なやり方で異なる素材を組み合わせていました。住宅の外観は白で統一されていて、黄色い枠の窓があります。ところが内部に入ると大理石と木が使われています。これらのエレメントは空間の体験に大きく影響してきます。装飾的なものとは違いますね。

　私はなにかほかのことを連想させる素材が好きです。アルド・ロッシ[11]の記憶の概念に近いかもしれません。都市の記憶ではなく純粋な記憶というのでしょうか、抽象的な建築は存在しないと思います。どんな建物であろうと、ほかの建物を連想させます。その建物のなかのほかの空間との関係もあります。それが素晴らしいのです。

GH　《バーゲンホフトのヴィラ》は、人間の生の歓びのようなものを大切にしている建築だと感じました。この人間の生に対する考え方は、あなたたちの建築思想の核心のひとつではないでしょうか。

KG　人間の生に関しては、私はダヴィッドから多くのことを学びました。私たちが出会う前、私は生に関して極端だったり快楽的だったりする、直接的な経験をしたことがありませんでした。そのような関心と異なるバックグラウンドのなかで育ったからです。ダヴィッドは、あらゆることに対して自由奔放な人間です。つね

に生きることを謳歌しています。彼の父はとても自由放任にダヴィッドを育てたのです。この事実と、私たちがロサンゼルスで学生だった頃に経験したことや魅了されたものが、建築の構造や思想以上のものをつくろうとする態度を形成したのです。それは生きることそのものでした。ロサンゼルスの土地柄に依るものなのかもしれません。

人生には曖昧なことが多くあります。起こることは起こるに任せることです。そういうものです。それを変えることはできません。その視点に立てば、人生は簡単なものです。

オフィスなしのオフィス

GH　最後に建築教育について訊かせてください。あなたはいまスイス連邦工科大学ローザンヌ校 (EPF Lausanne) で教鞭をとっています。教えることは好きですか？また大学で教えることとオフィスでの実務にはどのような関係があるのでしょうか。

KG　私は思考するために教えています。私が教える理由はそれだけです。ディスカッションをしたいのです。自分の建築だけを教える人がいますが、それは私のやり方ではありません。私は教えるとき、建築以外の話題を話します。でももちろん、ほかの話題を出すことは本当に伝えたいことを発見してもらうためのトリックであって、いわば、私が教えるときのコツです。けっこう気に入っています。

自分のモチヴェーションを高めてくれる人に会い続けることが大切です。優秀な学生に出会ったときには、彼らが快適になりすぎないようにすることが大事です。しかし、優秀な学生が少なくなっているのが残念です。いまは平均的な学生が多いですね。

教えていると、学生たちがあまり上達しないシチュエーションに遭うことがあります。それはそれでフラストレーションが溜まりますが、重要なことを議論できるかぎりにおいてはそれでも構わないと思っています。彼らに伝えようと工夫することで、自分が重要だと思っていることを問いなおすことになります。私たちが提案する建築は、いわゆる「ただの」建築ではありません。それを通じて自分自身を問いなおし続けたいのです。そうするために教えることはとても効果的です。教えることを通じて実際にそれをやらないといけないからです。また逆もあります。でも、教えるという行為は、結果としてあなたがやることとは無関係なのです。こだまのように響くかもしれませんが、完全に変えてしまうことはないでしょう。それは心地よいものです。教えるという行為はあなたに思考する機会を提供します。でも間

接的な影響です。私がスタジオで「オフィスなしのオフィス」という小さなブックレットをつくることにしたのはそのためです。そこは私にとって理想の場所で、自分の仕事をするけれども、コマーシャルな論理が排除された活動をする場所です。私はまだ市場から切り離された活動をすることが可能だと考えていて、そのことをテーマにしました。望むか望まないかはわかりませんが、そのときあなたは最もラディカルな建築家になれるし、そこでこそ商業的な成功にもつながる新しい価値が生み出されるでしょう。一方に（実務の場所としての）このオフィスがあります。そして教えることは、ある意味で私にとっては「オフィスなしのオフィス」なのかもしれないと思うようになりました。

GH 「オフィスなしのオフィス」。この対話を「オフィス」についての問いからはじめたので、ループして最初の問いに戻ったことになりますね。今日はありがとうございました。

1——エド・ルシェ（1937 -）：アメリカ出身の現代美術家。主な作品に《IF》（2000）や《Pay Nothing Until April》（2003）などがあり、文字を用いたコンセプチュアルな作風が特徴。
2——レム・コールハース（1944 -）：オランダ出身の建築家。70年代半ばに設計事務所OMA（Office for Metropolitan Architecture）を設立し、都市リサーチや出版を含めた幅広い活動を行なう。《ボルドーの住宅》（1998）、《シアトル中央図書館》（2004）などの建築作品のほか、主な著書に『錯乱のニューヨーク』（ちくま学芸文庫、1999、原著＝1978）や『S, M, L, XL』（010 Publishers、1995）がある。
3——ステファン・ベール（1955 -）：ベルギー出身の建築家。主な作品に《M邸》（1992）があるほか、ザヴェール・デ・ヘイテルと共同で《ゲント大学キャンパス増築計画》（2006）も手がけている。
4——ザヴェール・デ・ヘイテル（1957 -）：ベルギー出身の建築家。XDGA主宰。80年代はOMAのメンバーでもあった。主なプロジェクトにフランスの《サン・モーリス都市計画》（1996 -）、《シャッセーパーク・アパートメント》（2003）がある。
5—— MVRDV：90年代初頭に設立されたオランダの設計集団。設立者のヴィニー・マース（1959 -）、ヤコブ・ファン・ライス（1964 -）はOMA出身である。主な作品に《ハノーヴァー万博オランダ館》（2000）などがある。
6——アバロス＆ヘレロス：スペイン出身の建築家イニャキ・アバロス（1956 -）、ジョアン・ヘレロス（1958 -）による設計事務所。主な作品に《ウセラ公共図書館》（2002）がある。2008年に解散。
7——ロブレヒト・エン・ダーム：ベルギー出身の建築家ポール・ロブレヒト（1950 -）とヒルデ・ダーム（1950 -）による設計事務所。主な作品に《ブリュージュ・コンサートホール》（2002）、《マーケット・ホール》（2013）がある。
8——カルーゾ・セント・ジョン：アダム・カルーゾ（1962 -）とピーター・セント・ジョン（1959 -）によるイギリスの設計事務所。主な作品に《テート・ブリテンのミルバンク・プロジェクト》（2013）がある。
9——サージソン・ベイツ：ジョナサン・サージソン（1964 -）とスティーブン・ベイツ（1964 -）によるイギリスの設計事務所。主な作品に《ワンズワース工場の改装》（2004）、《リシン工芸センター》（2008）がある。
10——アドルフ・ロース（1870 - 1933）：オーストリア出身の建築家。装飾を排した建築外観、および三次元的な空間操作による独自の設計手法「ラウムプラン」が特徴。代表作に《ミュラー邸》（1930）、著作に『装飾と犯罪——建築・文化論集』（伊藤哲夫訳、中央公論美術出版、2011、原著＝1908）がある。
11——アルド・ロッシ（1931 - 97）：イタリア出身の建築家。主な作品に《ガララテーゼの集合住宅》（1973）、《世界劇場》（1979）があり、『都市の建築』（大島哲蔵＋福田晴虔訳、大龍堂書店、1991、原著＝1966）、『アルド・ロッシ自伝』（三宅理一訳、SD選書、1984、原著＝1981）などの著書を発表した。

対話を終えて | After the conversation

最後はベルギーのブリュッセルを拠点にするケルステン・ゲールスとダヴィッド・ファン・セーヴェレン。これまでベルギーは周囲の大国（フランス・オランダ・イギリス・ドイツ）の影に隠れて現代建築の知名度が低かったように思うが、近年になって若手建築家が注目を集めている。

「オフィス」という事務所名と、彼らのニュートラルでドライな作風は無関係ではないだろう。「水平的で民主的な」オフィスを目指しているとゲールスが言うとおり、ブリュッセル中心部にある彼らの事務所はリベラルな雰囲気に満ちている。僕が事務所に到着したとき、ちょうど締切り間近のコンペのプロジェクトについてゲールスとファン・セーヴェレンが険しい表情で激しい議論を戦わせていた。しかし議論を終えた瞬間、2人とも和やかな表情に変わり収録を始めようと僕に声をかけた。こうしたムードの切り替えの早さに、彼らがよいパートナーシップであることが窺えた。

対話では、彼らが学生時代に目撃した90年代のコールハースについての話が興味深かった。特に代表作となったフランスのプロジェクトにおいてコールハースの仕事は職人的かつ都市的であったという意味で、オランダ的というよりもベルギー的な建築家なのだというのはとても面白い指摘だ。ヨーロッパの中心にあるという地理的・文化的条件が、いまベルギーで職人的かつ都市的な建築をつくるコンテクストを可能にしている。そのことを2人は強く自覚していた。

彼らの作品には度々グリッドや列柱などの古典的な建築のエレメントが現われる。ファン・セーヴェレンが「古典的であることは、様式ではなく態度にかかわること」と言うように、これらのエレメントはある場所を把握

My final interview was with Kersten Geers and David Van Severen, based in Brussels. Until recently Belgium may have had a low profile in contemporary architecture, in the shadow of its larger neighbors (France, the Netherlands, the U.K., Germany). Nowadays, however, the country's younger architects are making a name for themselves.

The name of their office—"OFFICE"—and their dry, neutral architectural style are not unrelated. Located in central Brussels, the office has a truly liberal atmosphere, in keeping with what Geers describes as their aspiration to be "horizontal or democratic." When I arrived there, he and Van Severen wore stern expressions and were engaged in a vigorous argument about a project for a competition with a looming deadline. But as soon as they finished arguing, their expressions softened and they called out to me, "Let's start the conversation." The speed with which they were able to shift moods struck me as proof of a good partnership.

Of special interest to me in this interview was their discussion of Koolhaus, whose work they encountered in the 1990s during their student days. I was fascinated by the remark that Koolhaus was more of a Belgian than a Dutch architect, in the sense that his work was craftsmanlike and metropolitan, as exemplified by the projects in France for which he is best known. The geographical and cultural position of Belgium at the center of Europe provides the context today for the development there of architecture that has "craftsmanship with a metropolitan view." Geers and Van Severen are acutely aware of this.

In their work one often sees such classic

してコントロールするためのツールとして用いられている。ゲールスは「建築家ができることで最も重要なことはレファレンス、ガイドライン、定量化システムを示すことだ」と言った。彼らのこの明快な方法論はより大きな規模の建築でどのように展開されていくだろうか……などと思っていたら、この対話の収録後にローザンヌのスイス国営ラジオテレビ局複合施設「RTS Champ Continu」のコンペに勝利したという知らせが入った。SANAAの《Rolexラーニングセンター》の隣接地に建ち、35,000m²と彼らにとって最大プロジェクトになる。この規模で彼らが新しい境地を見せることを期待したい。

architectural elements as grids and colonnades. As David Van Severen put it, "Classic is not a style but an attitude," and they use these elements as tools to grasp and control a certain space. Geers further stated that "the most important thing you can do as an architect is introduce a set of references, a ruler, a measuring system." Hearing their words made me want to see how this clearly articulated methodology might translate to even larger-scale works. After the conversation I learned that they had won the commission for the RTS Champ Continu, a radio-TV station's media complex in Lausanne. Covering 35,000 square meters on a site next to SANAA's Rolex Learning Center, it is the largest project they have undertaken to date. I look forward to the new ground I'm sure they will break on this massive scale.

Kersten Geers & David Van Severen

スイス国営ラジオテレビ局複合施設／ローザンヌ、スイス／2014 −
RTS Champ Continu/Lausanne, Switzerland/2014-

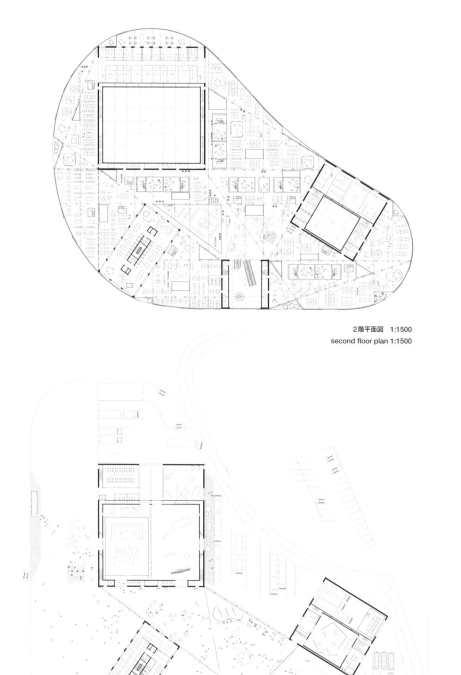

2階平面図　1:1500
second floor plan 1:1500

1階平面図　1:1500
first floor plan 1:1500

Kersten Geers & David Van Severen

Kersten Geers & David Van Severen

OFFICE 56 メルシュテムのウィークエンド・ハウス／ベルギー／2012
OFFICE 56 Weekend House in Merchtem/Belgium/2012

平面図 1:400
floor plan 1:400

Kersten Geers & David Van Severen

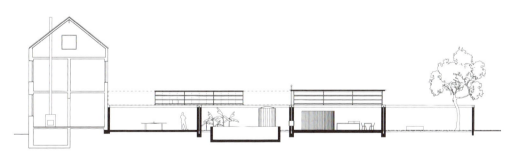

断面図 1:400
elevation 1:400

Kersten Geers & David Van Severen

Kersten Geers & David Van Severen

Kersten Geers & David Van Severen

OFFICE 39 バーゲンホフトのヴィラ／ベルギー／2010
OFFICE 39 Villa in Buggenhout/Belgium/2010

Kersten Geers & David Van Severen

Kersten Geers & David Van Severen

OFFICE 39 バーゲンホフトのヴィラ
OFFICE 39 Villa in Buggenhout

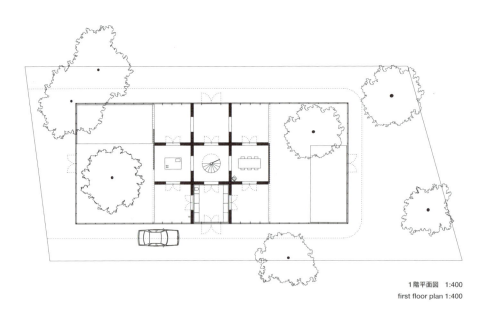

1階平面図 1:400
first floor plan 1:400

Kersten Geers & David Van Severen

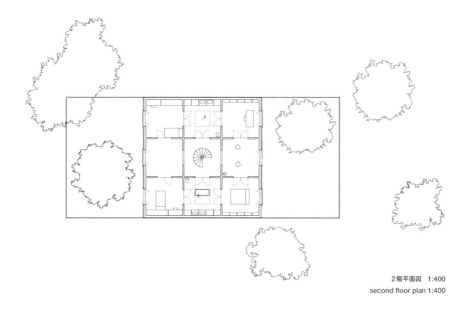

2階平面図　1:400
second floor plan 1:400

Kersten Geers & David Van Severen

略歴、編集・翻訳、図版クレジット

Biographies, Editing / Translation, Figure credits

略歴 | Biographies

長谷川豪

1977年埼玉県生まれ。2002年東京工業大学修士課程修了。2002–04年西沢大良建築設計事務所勤務を経て、2005年長谷川豪建築設計事務所設立。2009–11年東京工業大学ほか非常勤講師、2012–14年メンドリシオ建築アカデミー客員教授、2014年オスロ建築大学客員教授を務める。
著作＝『考えること、建築すること、生きること』（LIXIL出版、2011）、『Go Hasegawa 長谷川豪作品集』（TOTO出版、2012）、『石巻の鐘楼──ふたたび建てる建築』（誠文堂新光社、2012）

主な作品
2006　五反田の住宅
2010　練馬のアパートメント
2010　森のピロティ
2011　駒沢の住宅
2011　経堂の住宅
2012　石巻の鐘楼
2014　上尾の長屋
2014　御徒町のアパートメント

アルヴァロ・シザ

1933年ポルトガル、マトジニョシュ生まれ。1954年より設計活動を始める。1955年ポルト造形美術高等学校卒業。1955–58年までフェルナンド・ターヴォラと協働。1966–69年、76年からポルト大学建築学部教授。ハーヴァード大学、ペンシルヴァニア大学、スイス連邦工科大学ローザンヌ校客員教授を務める。1992年プリツカー賞、2012年ヴェネツィア・ビエンナーレ生涯功績に対する金獅子賞など受賞多数。

主な作品
1963　ボア・ノヴァ・レストラン（2014年改修）
1966　レサのスイミング・プール
1977　ボウサの集合住宅
1995　ポルト大学建築学部棟
1996　マルコ・デ・カナヴェーゼスの
　　　サンタ・マリア教会と教区センター
1997　セラルヴェス現代美術館
2008　イベレ・カマルゴ美術館
2009　ミメーシス美術館

ヴァレリオ・オルジャティ

1958年スイス、クール生まれ。スイス連邦工科大学チューリッヒ校で建築を学ぶ。1986年同大学卒業。チューリッヒ、ロサンゼルスの設計事務所で働いた後、1996年事務所を設立、2008年に妻のタマラとともにフリムスへ拠点を移す。2002年よりメンドリシオ建築アカデミーで教鞭をとる。2009年ハーヴァード大学客員教授。

主な作品
1998　パスペルスの小学校
1999　イエロー・ハウス
2005　K＋N邸
2007　リナード・バルディルのアトリエ
2008　スイス国立公園ビジターセンター
2010　プランタホフ農業学校の講堂
2012　ツーク・シュライフの集合住宅
2014　ヴィラ・アレム

ペーター・メルクリ

1953年スイス、チューリッヒ生まれ。スイス連邦工科大学チューリッヒ校で建築を学ぶ。高校時代、物理の教師に教えられた建築家ルドルフ・オルジャティに関心を抱き、彼から建築の基礎要素を学ぶ。スイス連邦工科大学チューリッヒ校在学中に彫刻家ハンス・ヨゼフソンを知り、彼のスタジオへ通うようになる。1978年チューリッヒに事務所を設立。2003年からスイス連邦工科大学チューリッヒ校の教授を務める。

主な作品
1982　2つの個人住宅
1992　彫刻の家
1997　エーレンバッハの住宅
2004　「イン・ビルヒ」総合制学校
2006　ノバルティス・キャンパス・ビジターセンター
2012　シンセスの新施設
2014　ホフ通りのガーデンハウス
2014　ベルヴォイル公園の料理学校

アンヌ・ラカトン

1955年フランス、サン=パルトゥー、ラ・リヴィエレ生まれ。1980年ボルドー建築学校卒業。1984年ボルドー大学にて都市計画の学位を取得後、1987年にジャン=フィリップ・ヴァッサルとラカトン&ヴァッサルを設立。2004年、2006年、2010-2011年にスイス連邦工科大学ローザンヌ校、2007-13年にマドリード建築技術学校で教授、2010年冬期パリスタジオ、ハーヴァード大学客員教授を務める。現在ハーヴァード大学客員教授。

ジャン=フィリップ・ヴァッサル

1954年モロッコ、カサブランカ生まれ。1980年ボルドー建築学校卒業後、アフリカ、ニジェールで建築家、都市計画家を務める。2002-06年、ヴェルサイユ建築学校で教鞭をとる。2012年よりベルリン芸術大学客員教授。

主な作品
- 1993　ラタピ邸
- 1998　キャップ・フェレのD邸
- 2001　パレ・ド・トーキョー（第一期：2001、第二期：2012）
- 2008　ナント建築学校
- 2011　ボワ・ル・プレートル高層住宅の改修
  　　　（フレデリック・デュルオーと協働）
- 2013　ノース・カレーの現代美術センター
- 2014　ネパートの59戸の庭付き住居
- 2014　パリ110戸の学生寮と30戸の住居

パスカル・フラマー

1973年スイス、フリブール生まれ。スイス連邦工科大学チューリッヒ校、デルフト工科大学、スイス連邦工科大学ローザンヌ校で建築を学ぶ。2001年スイス連邦工科大学チューリッヒ校にて学位取得。1998-2005年ヴァレリオ・オルジャティに師事。2005年より自身の設計活動をはじめる。同年よりスイス技術者・建築家協会（SIA）メンバー。メンドリシオ建築アカデミー、ハーヴァード大学、アムステルダムのサンドバーグ工科大学で教師を務める。現在はスイス連邦工科大学チューリッヒ校にて教鞭をとる。

主な作品
- 2000　2つの階段のあるオフィス
- 2005　フリオ・オトニのコミュニティ・センター
- 2007-12　バルシュタールの住宅
- 2009-15　リグーリアの住宅（マルタ・カサグランデと協働）
- 2012　フランクフルトの森のなかの住宅
- 2012　30戸のアパートメント（ソフラブ・サファリと協働）
- 2012　アーティストと家族のための斜面に建つ住宅
- 2013　ハリス・スカイ島のみえる住宅

ケルステン・ゲールス

1975年ベルギー、ヘント生まれ。ヘント大学、マドリード建築技術学校で建築・都市計画を学ぶ。ロッテルダムのマクスワン都市建築設計事務所、ノイントリング・リーダイク・アーキテクツに勤務した後、2002年にダヴィッド・ファン・セーヴェレンとオフィス・ケルステン・ゲールス・ダヴィッド・ファン・セーヴェレンを設立。ヘント大学教授、コロンビア大学客員教授、メンドリシオ建築アカデミー、スイス連邦工科大学ローザンヌ校で教鞭を取る。

ダヴィッド・ファン・セーヴェレン

1978年ベルギー、ヘント生まれ。ヘント大学、マドリード建築技術学校で建築・都市計画を学ぶ。ステファン・ベール・アーキテクツ、ザヴェール・デ・ギュイター・アーキテクツ、マールテン・ヴァン・セーヴェレン・アトリエに勤務。アムステルダム・アカデミー、デルフト工科大学、ロッテルダム・ベラーヘ研究所などで教師、ゲスト・クリティークを務める。現在ヴェルサイユ建築学校ゲスト・チューター。

主な作品
- 2003　OFFICE 2 アントワープのエントランス
- 2007　OFFICE 7 ゲントのサマーハウス
- 2010　OFFICE 39 バーゲンホフトのヴィラ
- 2010　OFFICE 47 ティルトのコンピュータ・ショップ
- 2010　OFFICE 85 ガーデン・パヴィリオン
  　　　（2010年ヴェネツィア・ビエンナーレでの
  　　　インスタレーション、バス・プリンセンと協働）
- 2012　OFFICE 56 メルシュテムのウィークエンド・ハウス
- 2012　OFFICE 62 ブリュッセルのシティ・ヴィラ
- 2014　OFFICE 90 ルーヴェンの農業学校

Biographies

Go Hasegawa

Go Hasegawa was born in Saitama, Japan in 1977. He completed the master course at the Graduate School of Science and Engineering, Tokyo Institute of Technology in 2002. In 2002-04 he worked at Taira Nishizawa Architects. He established Go Hasegawa & Associates in 2005. He was an adjunct lecturer at Tokyo Institute of Technology (2009-11) and elsewhere, and a visiting professor at the Academy of Architecture in Mendrisio in 2012-14 and the Oslo School of Architecture and Design in 2014.

Publications: *Thinking, Making Architecture, Living*, LIXIL Publishing, 2011; *Go Hasegawa—Works*, TOTO, 2012; *The Belfry in Ishinomaki, The Architecture Rebuild*, Seibundo Shinkosha, 2012

Selected Works

2006	House in Gotanda
2010	Apartment in Nerima
2010	Pilotis in a Forest
2011	House in Komazawa
2011	House in Kyodo
2012	Belfry in Ishinomaki
2014	Row House in Ageo
2014	Apartment in Okachimachi

Álvaro Siza

Álvaro Siza was born in Matozinhos, Portugal in 1933. He opened his private practice in Porto in 1954. He graduated from the Escola Superior de Belas-Artes do Porto in 1955, and worked with Fernando Távora in 1955-58. He has been a professor at the University of Porto in 1966-69, 76-; and visiting professor at the Harvard University Graduate School of Design, the University of Pennsylvania, and the Swiss Federal Institute of Technology Lausanne. He received the Prizker Prize in 1992, and received the Golden Lion for lifetime achievement at the Venice Biennale 2012.

Selected Works

1963	Boa Nova Tea House (transformed in 2014)
1966	Swimming Pool in Leça
1977	Social Housing in Bouça
1995	Faculty of Architecture, University of Porto
1996	Santa Maria Church in Marco de Canaveses and Parochial Center
1997	Serralves Museum of Contemporary Art Porto
2008	Iberê Camargo Foundation
2009	Mimesis Museum

Valerio Olgiati

Valerio Olgiati was born in Chur, Switzerland in 1958. He studied architecture at the Swiss Federal Institute of Technology Zürich, and graduated in 1986. Having lived and worked in Zürich and Los Angeles, he established his own practice in 1996 in Zurich, and in 2008 together with his wife Tamara in Flims. He is a professor at the Academy of Architecture in Mendrisio since 2002. He held the Kenzo Tange chair at Harvard University in 2009.

Selected Works

1998	School in Paspels
1999	The Yellow House
2005	K+N Residence
2007	Atelier Bardill
2008	Swiss National Park Visitor Center
2010	Plantahof Auditorium
2012	Residential Building Zug Schleife
2014	Villa Além

Peter Märkli

Peter Märkli was born in Zürich, Switzerland in 1953, and studied architecture at the Swiss Federal Institute of Technology Zürich. While he was in high school his physics teacher drew his attention to the architect Rudolf Olgiati, who taught him to recognize the basic elements of architecture. While he was at the Swiss Federal Institute of Technology Zürich he got to know the sculptor Hans Josephsohn and began to visit his studio regularly. He set up his studio in Zürich in 1978. He is a professor at the Swiss Federal Institute of Technology Zürich since 2003.

Selected Works

1982	Two Single Houses
1992	La Congiunta
1997	Single-family House in Erlenbach
2004	"Im Birch" Comprehensive School
2006	Novartis Campus Visitor Center
2012	Neubau Synthes
2014	Garden House Hochstrasse
2014	School of Gastronomy, Belvoirpark

Anne Lacaton

Anne Lacaton was born in Saint Pardoux la Rivière, France in 1955. She obtained her diploma at the Architecture School of Bordeaux in 1980, and her diploma in city planning at the University of Bordeaux in 1984. She co-founded Lacaton & Vassal in 1987 with Jean-Philippe Vassal. She has been a professor at the Swiss Federal Institute of Technology Lausanne in 2004, 2006, and 2010-11; and the Superior Technical School of Architecture of Madrid (2007-13). She has been a visiting professor at the Harvard University Graduate School of Design in Paris winter studio of 2010-11 and is currently at the Harvard Graduate School of Design in Boston (2015).

Jean-Philippe Vassal

Jean-Philippe Vassal was born in Casablanca, Morocco in 1954. He obtained his diploma at the Architecture School of Bordeaux in 1980. In 1980-85 he worked as architect and city planner in Niger. He has been visiting professor at the Architecture School of Versailles (2002-06); Peter Behrens School of Architecture, Düsseldorf (summer 2005); Technical University of Berlin (2007-10); and Swiss Federal Institute of Technology Lausanne (2010-11). He has been professor at the Berlin University of the Arts since 2012.

Selected Works

1993	Latapie House
1998	D House in Lége-Cap-Ferret
2001	Palais de Tokyo (phase one: -2001, phase two: -2012)
2008	School of Architecture in Nantes
2011	Bois-le-Prétre Tower Block Transformation (with Frederic Druot)
2013	FRAC Nord-Pas de Calais
2014	59 Dwellings in Neppert Gardens
2014	30 Dwellings and 110 Student Dwellings in Paris

Pascal Flammer

Pascal Flammer was born in Fribourg, Switzerland in 1973. He studied architecture at the Swiss Federal Institute of Technology Zürich, Delft University of Technology, and Swiss Federal Institute of Technology Lausanne. He obtained his diploma at the Swiss Federal Institute of Technology Zürich as a Master of Science in Architecture in 2001. He worked with Valerio Olgiati in 1998-2005 and started his own practice in 2005. He is a member of the Swiss Engineers and Architects Association (SIA) since 2005. He has taught at the Academy of Architecture in Mendrisio, at the Harvard University Graduate School of Design, and at the Sandberg Institute in Amsterdam. He is currently teaching at the Swiss Federal Institute of Technology Zürich.

Selected Works

2000	Office with Two Stairs, Zürich
2005	Centro Comunitário Júlio Otoni, Rio de Janeiro
2007-12	House in Balsthal
2009-15	House in Liguria (with Marta Casagrande)
2012	House in a Forest, Frankfurt am Main
2012	30 Apartments, Berlin (with Sohrab Zafari)
2012	House on a Slope for an Artist and Family
2013	House with View on Isle of Skye, Harris

Kersten Geers

Kersten Geers was born in Ghent, Belgium in 1975. He graduated in Architecture and Urbanism from the University of Ghent and the ETSA Madrid. He worked with Maxwan Architects and Urbanists and with Neutelings Riedijk Architects in Rotterdam. He co-founded OFFICE Kersten Geers David Van Severen in 2002 with David Van Severen. He has been a professor at the University of Ghent, visiting professor at Columbia University and at the Academy of Architecture in Mendrisio, and is currently teaching at the Swiss Federal Institute of Technology Lausanne.

David Van Severen

David Van Severen was born in Ghent, Belgium in 1978. He graduated in Architecture and Urbanism from the University of Ghent and the ETSA Madrid. He worked with Stéphane Beel Architects, Xaveer De Geyter Architects, and Atelier Maarten Van Severen. He has been a teacher and guest critic at the Academy of Amsterdam, the Delft University of Technology, and the Berlage Institute in Rotterdam, and he is currently guest tutor at the Architecture School of Versailles.

Selected Works

2003	OFFICE 2 Entrance in Antwerp
2007	OFFICE 7 Summer House in Ghent
2010	OFFICE 39 Villa in Buggenhout
2010	OFFICE 47 Computer Shop in Tielt
2010	OFFICE 85 Garden Pavilion (Installation for Venice Architecture Biennale 2010, in collaboration with Bas Princen)
2012	OFFICE 56 Weekend House in Merchtem
2012	OFFICE 62 City Villa in Brussels
2014	OFFICE 90 Agriculture School in Leuven

編集・翻訳 | Editing / Translation

アルヴァロ・シザとの対談
協力：レベッカ・プロジ、ティナ・キュング
収録支援：マニュエル・モンテネグロ、
ロドリゴ・ダ・コスタ・リマ
英語編集：クリストファー・ステイヴンス
日本語翻訳：牧尾晴喜

Conversation with Álvaro Siza
Cooperation: Rebecca Ploj, Tina Küng
Support: Manuel Montenegro,
Rodrigo da Costa Lima
English Editing: Christopher Stephens
Translation: Haruki Makio

ヴァレリオ・オルジャティとの対談
協力：マクシミリアン・トレイバー、
ベアトリーチェ・カロリーナ・ガンバート
英語編集：クリストファー・ステイヴンス
日本語翻訳：牧尾晴喜

Conversation with Valerio Olgiati
Cooperation: Maximilian Treiber,
Beatrice Carolina Gambato
English Editing: Christopher Stephens
Translation: Haruki Makio

ペーター・メルクリとの対談
協力：ベアロッハー太央、
マクシミリアン・トレイバー
英語編集：アラン・グリースン
日本語翻訳：牧尾晴喜

Conversation with Peter Märkli
Cooperation: Baerlocher Tao, Maximilian Treiber
English Editing: Alan Gleason
Translation: Haruki Makio

アンヌ・ラカトン＆
ジャン=フィリップ・ヴァッサルとの対談
協力：ルーカス・フィンク
英語編集：アラン・グリースン
日本語翻訳：牧尾晴喜

Conversation with Anne Lacaton & Jean-Philippe Vassal
Cooperation: Lucas Fink
English Editing: Alan Gleason
Translation: Haruki Makio

パスカル・フラマーとの対談
協力：アン・ファン・ハウト、
フィリップ・メシュコ
英語編集：スーザン・ロジャース・竹馬
日本語翻訳：堀口徹

Conversation with Pascal Flammer
Cooperation: Anne van Hout and Filip Mesko
English Editing: Susan Rogers Chikuba
Translation: Tohru Horiguchi

ケルステン・ゲールス＆
ダヴィッド・ファン・セーヴェレン
協力：フィリップ・メシュコ
英語編集：スーザン・ロジャース・竹馬
日本語翻訳：堀口徹

Conversation with Kersten Geers & David Van Severen
Cooperation: Filip Mesko
English Editing: Susan Rogers Chikuba
Translation: Tohru Horiguchi

図版クレジット ｜ Figure credits

長谷川豪	pp. 010-011, 018, 033, 041, 047, 054-055, 060, 089, 102, 127, 131, 144, 173, 186, 213, 228, 257
Álvaro Siza Archive	pp. 027, 032, 034, 036-037, 040, 044, 048, 049, 050, 052, 053 上下, 056, 057
Pedro Coutinho	pp. 035, 042, 051
Paulo Sousa	p. 043
Creative Commons	p. 045
maloutte	p. 073
Javier Miguel Verme	pp. 074-075, 076, 079, 080-081
Archive Olgiati	pp. 078, 082, 083, 090, 091, 092, 093, 094-095, 096-097, 098, 099 上下
Dennis Jarvis	pp. 084, 085
Peter Märkli Architekt	pp. 114, 117, 126, 134, 135
Caroline Palla	pp. 116, 140, 141
Goran Potkonjak	pp. 119, 136, 137 上下
©2015 Succession H.Matisse/SPDA, Tokyo	p. 120
Margherita Spiluttini	p. 122
Heinrich Helfenstein	pp. 124-125
Paolo Rosselli	pp. 132-133
Kati Deér	p. 138-139
Lacaton & Vassal	pp. 156, 158 上下, 163, 174, 175, 176 上, 178, 180
Philippe Ruault	pp. 160-161, 164-165, 167, 176 下, 177, 179, 181 上下, 182-183
Hans-Ulrich Obrist ed., *Re: CP by Cedric Price*, Birkhäuser, 2002　p. 166	
Gabriel de Andrade Fernandes	p. 199
Pascal Flammer Architect	pp. 200, 201, 206, 207, 214, 215, 216, 218, 224, 225
Ioana Marinescu	pp. 202-203, 217, 219 上下, 220, 221, 222-223
vince42	p. 204
OFFICE Kersten Geers David Van Severen	pp. 237, 241, 245, 255, 258, 259, 260 下, 261 下 266 下, 267 下
Bas Princen	pp. 246-247, 248 上下, 250-251, 260 上, 261 上, 262-263, 264-265, 266 上, 267 上
Iwan Baan	p. 252

p. 206 絵画	Félix Vallotton, *La Blanche et la Noire*, 1913
	Félix Vallotton, *Nu Endormi*, 1908
p. 207 絵画	Félix Vallotton, *Femme au Parroquet*, 1909
	Félix Vallotton, *Nu couché au Tapis Rouge*, 1909

長谷川豪　カンバセーションズ
ヨーロッパ建築家と考える現在と歴史

発行日：　　　2015年3月10日第1刷発行
　　　　　　　2020年1月20日第3刷発行

著者：　　　　長谷川豪、アルヴァロ・シザ、ヴァレリオ・オルジャティ、ペーター・メルクリ、
　　　　　　　アンヌ・ラカトン & ジャン・フィリップ・ヴァッサル、パスカル・フラマー、
　　　　　　　ケルステン・ゲールス & ダヴィッド・ファン・セーヴェレン

発行者：　　　ジン・ソン・モンテサーノ
発行所：　　　LIXIL出版
　　　　　　　〒104-0031　東京都中央区京橋3-6-18
　　　　　　　TEL 03-5250-6571　FAX 03-5250-6549　https://www.livingculture.lixil/publish/

企画・編集・制作：飯尾次郎、出原日向子（speelplaats co., ltd.）
英語編集協力：　　アラン・グリースン、クリストファー・ステイヴンス、
　　　　　　　　　スーザン・ロジャース・竹馬、テランス・レジェテ
日本語翻訳：　　　堀口徹、牧尾晴喜
デザイン：　　　　色部義昭、加藤亮介（株式会社日本デザインセンター 色部デザイン研究室）
印刷：　　　　　　株式会社 加藤文明社

ISBN978-4-86480-016-7 C0052
©2015 by Go Hasegawa
Printed in Japan

乱丁・落丁本はLIXIL出版までお送りください。送料小社負担にてお取り替えいたします。